PUZZLED

when the Pieces don't

seem to Fit

an

Autism Awareness
Anthology

inner child press, ltd.

General Information

PUZZLED

When The Pieces Don't Seem To Fit

Anthology

1st Edition : 2013

This Publishing is protected under Copyright Law as a "Collection". All rights for all submissions are retained by the Individual Author and or Artist. No part of this Publishing may be Reproduced, Transferred in any manner without the prior *WRITTEN CONSENT* of the "Material Owner" or its Representative Inner Child Press. Any such violation infringes upon the Creative and Intellectual Property of the Owner pursuant to International and Federal Copyright Law. Any queries pertaining to this "Collection" should be addressed to Publisher of Record.

Publisher Information
1st Edition : Inner Child Press :
intouch@innerchildpress.com
www.innerchildpress.com

This Collection is protected under U.S. and International Copyright Laws

Copyright © 2013 : Poets and Writers for Autism Awareness and Acceptance

ISBN-13 : 978-0615798905
ISBN-10 : 061579890X

$ 17.95

Always
Unique
Totally
Intelligent
Sometimes
Mysterious

Dedication

This Book is dedicated to my Sun Jude and all the Beautiful and Gifted Children and Adults like him.

Be brave, be bold, be smart, be curious, be happy, be sensitive, be gifted, just be UNIQUELY you....HUMAN

~YB

Preface

The Poetic Anthology *"Puzzled...When the Pieces Don't Seem to Fit"* was born from a need to bring awareness and acceptance to Autism Spectrum Disorder, a Neurological Disorder that affects social and communication development. ASD crosses all ethnic and socioeconomic lines, affecting 2-4 per 10,000 births in which boys are 4 times as likely to be diagnosed than girls, which means 1 in every 70 boys are diagnosed as having Autism. The "Spectrum" as it is commonly called, can range in expression from severely involved to mildly affected.

I being the Mother of a "Sun" who is on the spectrum wanted to do something to bring insight to help empower advocacy in a way that most had not. While my experience is different from others, there are many children and adults living with Autism who struggle with support and not having the voice to convey their thoughts or feelings of being "different not less." With that notion myself along with Marquise Williams reached out to our Poetic Community of beautifully talented friends and associates to help give a voice to a very misunderstood and commonly misdiagnosed disorder. We've found that the 6 degrees of separation where Autism is concerned within our Poetic community is astounding. It is our hope that this is the perfect way to contribute by offering a collection of Poetry containing pieces written by Artists directly or indirectly affected by Autism.

We came together collectively using our gift of words as only we as Poets/Writers and Artists know how, to impact awareness and promote education and acceptance of a Disorder that affects myself and countless others.

Whether you Love someone or just know someone who knows someone else with some form of Autism, we hope to honor them by bringing a level of consciousness to this disorder that is so prevalent and widely misunderstood in our society.

Please enjoy these wonderful works of poetry and prose beautifully written in our words from a different perspective in *"Puzzled....When the Pieces Don't Seem to Fit."*

Foreword

Affectionately called Solace, my daughter Maya used to smile like the sun with her eyes. At 12 months of age, she would stare at me with this deep understanding that, although she still could not speak, she yelled with triumph against all odds. Her excited little fingers would dance around objects with tactile familiarity; and I could almost hear through her giggly squeal, the blossoming of a little girl with a bright future.

But, like many parents with my concerns, in the still of the night when my brain tried to wrap around the constant why's and how come's, I wondered if my ray of hope would ever get the chance to express herself in ways that I could understand better…in ways that other parents took for granted: "I want milk", "Mommy, I'm sleepy"….or maybe just, "I love you".

Autism affects nearly 2 to 4 per 10,000 births. As a spectral condition, children are diagnosed based on their levels of cognitive, physical, and behavioral abilities. Although current research is in its baby stages, the grassroots and outreach phenomenon that has surrounded the cause has been nothing short of amazing. Between walks and runs, telethons, carnivals, and parades designed to raise both money and awareness, autism is embraced and supported by more and more people daily.

Puzzled…When the Pieces Don't Seem to Fit is a part of this community outreach. This book brings autism and its effects to the personal level through the heartfelt and poignant words of several poets who have been directly and indirectly affected by it. It is an outcry of courage and compassion; a communion of hopes, dreams, and ambition through verse and prose. This book challenges those who know very little about autism to raise their own voices, and those who do to continue to hold the banner higher.

I never treated Maya's diagnosis of autism as a disability, and 'till this day at the beautiful age of 11, Maya does not see herself as having one. Rather, I have always explained to Maya that she simply sees the world with a different set of colors. As a vibrant and aspiring artist, she dowses her reality with these hues through art. She paints the visions of "I love you" that I once thought she couldn't comprehend.

When you read this book, I urge you to get involved. Contact your local autism organizations, participate in an autism walk or run, initiate conversations about it within your own circles of friends, family, and associates. We all can play a part in furthering the research and education of others by actively becoming advocates, so that the pieces of this intricate puzzle called autism can be further understood.

Isis Sun

Table of Contents

Preface	vi
Foreword	vii

The Poets

Nicole Scates-Mackey	1
Yvette Burks	3
Yvette Burks	4
Quise Williams	6
Mizz Fab	7
Andrew Scott	9
ShiShi Venus	11
Vicki Aquah	12
Mister 668	13
Yvette Burks	16
Lisa N. Wiley	18
Isly Mo	19
Kelligraphy Pens	21
Andrew Scott	22
Jamie Bond	24

*T*able of *C*ontents... *continued*

Quise Williams	26
Starr Poetress	27
Stuart Irving Marshall	29
Quise Williams	31
Jacqueline Thomas Rome	33
Lion Heart	35
Planted Daisies	36
Samuel Rain Benjamin	38
Ashley Diaz McDaniel	40
Patrick Read	43
Krystal Davis	45
Linda Terrell	48
Isolda McClelland	52
Carla Howard-Danies	54
Justin Toney	55
Carlene Beverly	57
Blaq Diamond	58
Gail Weston Shazor	60
Mimi T. Davis	63
David Colvert	64

Table of Contents ... *continued*

Gabe Moses	68
Janet P. Caldwell	70
William S. Peters, Sr.	71
Yvette Burks	74

Pictures & Graphics — 77
Epilogue — 89

In Other Words by Yvette Burks	90
Articles and Information	93
What Is Autism	94
How is Autism Diagnosed	99
Symptoms	104
How is Autism Treated	114
Autism and your Family	118
Facts about Autism	132
Asperger's Syndrome	133
World Autism Awareness Day	144
Resources	145
Books for Children	149
Acknowledgments	150

PUZZLED

when the Pieces don't

seem to Fit

an
Autism Awareness
Anthology

inner child press, ltd.

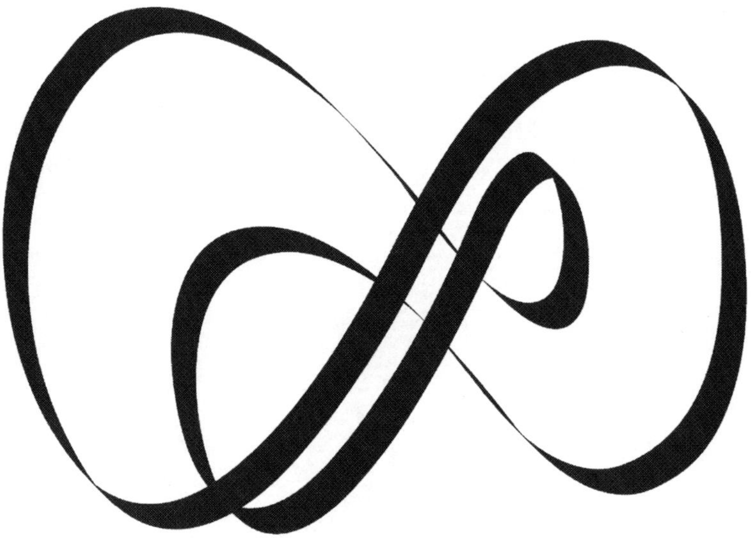

In His Image

Dear God,
I pray that people can see me.
That they would stop looking past me
as if autism defines me.
Allow them to see my strengths, the things that I excel in.
They only seem to see what they determine I lack,
the things that they see that sets me apart
from being "normal."
Don't they know the world needs different?
I am a designer's original, handcrafted by Your very hands.
You told me You broke the mold with me,
created in Your image.
You saw fit to choose me to be
 the piece of the puzzle that though
It's not quite shaped like the others…
without me it could not be completed.
Lord open their eyes that they may see
one of your greatest creations.
No, I don't go with the masses.
I'm very honest.
I don't pretend to be something I'm not.
I don't fake to like what I don't,
nor say what I don't mean and feel…
even though I may not be able to express it like others.
I am a soul.
A three part being; spirit, body & soul.
Just like them.
And words and actions affect me the same.
Lord don't let them put me in a box.
For there is no limit to the things
I can accomplish with you.

an Autism Awareness Anthology

Every limitation, boundary, bar,
dam can get bull-dozed by my drive.
After all I was made in Your image.
Don't let them treat me differently,
nor allow them to ignore my growth
Or my process, belittle my triumphs,
or impede it with their pity, unbelief
Or lack of faith in the beauty of You in me.
I can do anything.
Let no one give up on me.
I am fearfully and wonderfully made.
I am a gift.
A beautiful surprise to this world.
The puzzle piece that completes it.
Lord I pray that they would see me,
Beyond what they label me.

~ Nicole Scates-Mackey

Haiku

Emotionless stares

Spectrum of many colors

Autism Speaks....LOUD

Yvette Burks

Timothy

I remember being carried
High a top shoulders
With life swirling around
Totally oblivious to the lesson
I was being prepared for
You…my mother's baby brother
Carried me this way every single day
With no complaints, in fact you made it
You're priority
As I grew and matured past the Grand Canyon
Of years that separated us
I realized that you remained the same
Seeming to have aged physically, but not
Mentally or so I thought
I soon found out that your mental capacity
Was just "different…not less"
All the years of watching you write in
Those notebooks and tablets
Started to make sense to me now
Your ability to recall any sports stats had
Become something that I took pride in telling
My friends about, I started seeing it as a gift
Like who could really do this kind of
Thing if they weren't gifted right?
I could imagine numbers floating around
In your head like some sort of Matrix
In which only you can decipher the codes
But most didn't see it in that way
Because when you were born there was
No name for this gift or this affliction
As some would call it
There was either you were this or that
So you were stamped with a negative label
Giving anyone who saw you tunnel vision
No looking from their peripheral view

PUZZLED ~ When the Pieces don't see to Fit

Any one who knew, you knew of
Your affinity for sports stats
Almost having total recall and if the
Facts seemed to escape you, which
Was almost never, you knew the exact
Location in those crates where to find
The answers you were seeking
Most were quite fascinated by it
I was alway amazed by your diligence
There was always a pattern for them
When I looked at the page it all
Just looked the same
In hindsight I realize that your
Gift was a setup for the gift I
Received later on in my life
So now that Granny is gone
And you need more assistance
Just as you carried me
It is my turn to help
Carry you

~Yvette Burks

an Autism Awareness Anthology

Gifted

My mind...
Although to you, may seem to spin
On its axis in a cul-de-sac's one way in and out
But the difference is, the way you envision and
The ways that I'm gifted are far from one in the same
No, there's no one to blame
I am as I was born to be
God gifted me with limited speech
So that you can see
So, you can feel
This kaleidoscope of color that can't be found
In any box of Crayons in which, I see on a daily basis
To go through the motions of emotions only to be a teacher
Of patience and understanding
To make you understand that
I see and understand things in ways
you can't begin to fathom
When even, you think I don't
Overhead projected,
developed in the darkroom of my mind so
You may see the spotlight in which I shine
The only difference is, there is no difference in me
I am only as I was born to be
Gifted

~ Quise Williams

Who Let You In

who let you in
with your mud boots
and grimy fingerpaint fingers
trampling up and down Cerebral halls
shouting the annoying song as loud as you can
who let you in
destroying this sanctuary i built with my two hands
turning every damn light on in the house
jumping on the furniture
don't you have any sense
multiplying before my eyes
your voices magnified
begging for a time out
i won't rock you to sleep
sing you lullabies through another temper tantrum
you will not sit there eating sugar cereal
watching cartoons at 4 a.m.
sneaking over to my caged memories
wishing to pick the lock
just to get a peak
who let you in
with your back packs full of emotions
careful placed like misplaced gradeschool art
i tried to magic eraser you away
but you are here to stay
leaving me dwelling on my flaws
we both found corners
and demanded final snack pack pudding cup
before throwing our hands up in surrender
lost and found security blankets
tattered up
passed out anywhere but bed
dreaming of wonderwoman
destroying dinosaurs with laser eyes
seconds before the world exploded

we where dreamers once
before dreaming wasn't cool
now these children only come out at midnight
race around the same Cerebral halls
sometimes wishing to be princess for the day
anything but strong
even though capable of cleaning up messes
today she wants to sit this one out
lay sprawled out on the floor
coloring out the lines
making the most outrageous masterpieces inside a fort
today she doesn't want to share herself with the world
she wants to be alone
hoarding all the legos and g.i. joes
today she wants to find herself in those piece of trash art
prove to one person she can fly
fast and free
today she wants to get rid of the noise
the spinning in her head
knowing the one who let all her mess in
must send this party home......

~ Mizz Fab

God's Special Child

Loved, unloved when he came out of the womb
Seeing the light and the darkness of life's tomb
So young when he was asked to understand
The dealing of life's wrong hand

Bright eyed and bushy tailed
Little child innocence when he wailed
The simple joy of learning
Left his soft smiling

God's special child liked to discover
Every day's wonder
Invent new games for hours
Giving himself powers

He did this every day without motherly love
She left when push came to shove
Ignored day after day, while he was playing blocks
Still wearing last week's socks

God's special child went without proper education
The was never quick enough to ask the right question
Never knowing what was right or wrong
Never cowing how to get along

With a tear, his hands were always held out
Trying to find out what this loneliness was all about
Was it him that put the people in such a state?
Was it that his mind was not straight?

His world and heart was full of potential
You cannot measure what is internal
Hidden beneath childhood cries
The boy became a man before your very eyes

God's special child was continuously knocked down
Being met with other's frowns
What they did not see or know
Was the spiritual glow

The glorious strength that rests in him
Other predicting his upcoming life being grim
But every day, he faces the downside
Carrying himself with pride

There is no end for his light
You can see his heart burn night after night
When he reaches his mountain, he will do it in style
He is God's special child

~ Andrew Scott – Just a Maritime Boy

My Angel My Life

In my womb I felt your touch
you talk with me before you arrived
when our eye mirrored each other for the first time
to my surprise your beauty took my breath away
I never knew that first embrace
would melt my heart and tear my face
a miracle blessing came just for me
through my father a gift from God almighty
so now that we have become as one
thanking heaven while I raise you to the sun
giving praise for all the days we've bond
played and sang your favorite song
my angel my life
the treasure of my joy
throughout eternity you're my baby boy

~Shihi Venus

an Autism Awareness Anthology

Disconnected

I wish my child could write a poem
and open up his channels
I need my channels open too
because no ones talking to me.
My loved ones and disliked
ones whom have made their
transition, none of them will talk to me,
they pay me no attention.
I need communication, from the other side.
I got channels to open, no ones talking to me...not even
my child. They gave my child a vaccination,
which was so sadistic, they knew this batch of
medicine could leave my child Autistic.
So I called upon the ancestors to help
communicate. My babies like a zombie,
there's no light in his eyes.
They told me that
he'd be just fine, but they were telling lies.
The side affects were harmful, more harmful
than the cure, I hate what I am thinking now, I
know my thoughts impure. My child is now a
prisoner he is buried deep within
no wit, personality or charm.....That dag-Blasted
Vaccination has caused my baby harm!
I would love to hear the voice of my disconnected
child, I call upon my ancestors
but only the wind is blowing
Sadly I sit moping, alone. I
call upon my forefathers/and mothers...
I got channels to open I try to hold my child my
hug is rejected, I want to reach my baby
But he is now Dis-connected!

~Vicki Aquah

GIFTED

He speaks like an offbeat tune of raindrops
on a tin roof…and
If you listen carefully you can hear the sounds
of bottle rockets' red glare and bombs
bursting in air when his mind explodes
like pop rocks & gun shots and
and after his chaos calms…

You can see secrets nestled
behind his eyes all waiting for the chance to
bust like broken bottles against brick walls…like
a synapse of crashing cymbals in a symphony….but there's
nothing wrong here!!…THIS
was meant to be…so stop thinking of him
as an experiment gone wrong…
HE….is super concentrated…and WE are merely watered
down versions working only at
10% capacity.

He is a messenger of enigmatic thoughts of how's & whys
and what could be…see
God granted him access to understanding
Quadrants and Angles at 6
so he could navigate the stars…and rest his imagination
on the rings of Saturn…so
make no mistake he's more precise
than a Swiss timepiece and smarter than the average…
he bears the burden of being God's idea
of "difficult takes a day, impossible takes a week"…
and though he may appear weak in his social graces…
and to some it may seem like his
mental acuity is askew…but tell me…

When was the last time you went to college at 12 or
memorized every detail of a New
York skyline…after just a 20 minute view?

~ Mister668

PUZZLED ~ When the Pieces don't see to Fit

an Autism Awareness Anthology

Haiku

Kaleidoscope of

colors in cool and warm hues

colored beautiful

Yvette Burks

PUZZLED ~ When the Pieces don't see to Fit

an Autism Awareness Anthology

Through Keanu's Eyes

Alive with excitement and wonder yet

Unaffected by people's misguided views

They give me strange looks... Fail to see that

I am human

Special in God's eyes... A living

Testimony that angels exist

In this world, As well as in Heaven. God's

Creation... Perfectly unique

~LeeLee Aint Msbehavin' (aka) Lisa N. Wiley

FROM AIDEN

There will never be enough words
To describe exactly how beautiful
The world truly is
How each flap of a butterfly's wings
Makes the world shift a little on its axis
That a rainbow is proof
That everything I see
Can be as miraculous
As my inability to speak is
Because if you could hear
The gorgeous of my moans
The happiness that implodes in my grunts
The mercy that graces my scream
The amazing wonder of my shriek
Then you would understand
The lack of need to speak
And I know...
Sometimes you wish nothing more
For me than to bend words to my will
With ease like ropes
Untwisting from the twirl of a tire swing
But if you could watch
The clouds just ONCE and see
The magical movies playing just for me...
If you could travel through
The empires I built from the ground up
With only a few Lego blocks...
If you could bask
In the sheer enjoyment
Of the simple things
Like the breeze...
And the way it reminds me
Of the first time
You kissed my cheek

an Autism Awareness Anthology

The exact moment I knew
The infinite amount of love
You would forever rain over me
At times
I find myself
Singing praises
To your name
Into the fan
In hymn-like refrains
That I wish you could understand...
And sometimes
...A scream
Is the only thing
I have to offer
Because there would never
Be enough words
To tell anyone
How miraculous the world is
The way I see everything in it
How the bloom of a flower
Is as impressive as the sunrise
And how awesome it is to see
That it's all so intricately connected
Then you'd see
How trivial the need to speak is
Because there is sooo much
Beauty in the things that can only be seen by me
And I wish...I could invite you into
The fantasy that my eyes and ears
Embark on every day...
But I'm sorry Mommy...
There will never be
The right words
For me to explain.

~Isly Mo

PUZZLED ~ When the Pieces don't see to Fit

I Love You Mommy

She lived inside herself
Heart pulsating to the beat
Of an internal rhyme scheme
Occasionally she'd peek into my eyes
Then die back into the blanketed comfort
Of her own skin
She'd listen to the clickety-clack
Of footsteps begging her to speak
Coercing her to release
Just one syllable
But her ill was her will
A prison of death sentences
With no living will
No pills could cure her
Still....I loved her
Though she lived inside herself
Trapped like 64 crayons in a box
She was a rainbow of padlocks
That kept her voice a wax secret
Museumed in a mold of Madam Tussauds
House of fame
Who was to blame for her silence?
This shimmering diamond
Who couldn't hide her screaming siren
Alone on her sand filled deserted island
I land on my knees
Pray for her eternal peace
I swear I lost a piece of me
When she drew a picture of me
Handed it to me silently
As if to say...I love you Mommy!!

~Kelligraphy Pens

an Autism Awareness Anthology

Wanna Go Home

I'm only twelve years old
Trapped in a room, with four walls that are so cold
Pacing around in circles everyday
Nobody to visit, nothing to say
Walls are an aged blue
Scraped all over. Memories of what others here have been through
Their screams coming out of the paint
Energy sapped until you feel faint
No one is taking care of me
No one else in this room, I see
Sitting in a corner, I am afraid
Trying to understand the person that has been made
What did I do to come to this prison?
Who played God and made this decision
No one said that I did something wrong
But I know I am different and most do not think I belong
Now I am in a place where everything just closes in
With thoughts that make me shake again and again
I am so alone with feelings that I do not understand
No one holding my open hand
I am only twelve years old
And I already know too much about the cold
I just sit here, letting just my mind roam
When I just wanna go home!

~ Andrew Scott – Just a Maritime Boy

PUZZLED ~ When the Pieces don't see to Fit

Christopher Alexander Wyatt

If we are here for a purpose
And everything happens for a reason
Then Autistic kids are a special gift
Because not everyone gets one
They are rare and personally assigned
As if God custom-made them
For the family circle who's acquired one
An autistic child is a unique blessing

The brilliance of their eyes trapped inside of a prism
Mind's eye moves a mile a minute
Smart beyond comprehension
Brain cells serving a lifetime sentence
Locked in the abyss of 10% of a minds prison

Communication skills of another language
Frustrated that you can't always understand them
And they move fast and speak slow
Just to help us comprehend
They stimulate our ability to communicate with them

They are a rare pipe organ that we cannot quite tune
Beautiful souls that nose-dived into a body too soon
In a breach position and we can't quite turn...
If the brain was a hat then imagine it not aligned exact
There is nothing wrong with them...
There is something about us ...
Pay close attention.... They are here to teach us

PUZZLED ~ When the Pieces don't see to Fit

Music lovers...
They find rhythms to frequencies we don't even hear
They see things in 3D, can count faster than you and me
With a photogenic memory that could rebuild the world

We have become creatures of habit
Re-learning how to co-exist in a world of active thinkers....
More than one mind and angle to think from ... parhelia
They are born with patience for us... not us for them....

Autism... Is a superpower...
NOT a disability ... it's a difference
We live outside they live inside of themselves...
They are the phenomena's of the mental spectrum
Synesthesia prodigies ...they taste everything...
Colors, scents, lights, pictures,
Even emotions before you have them
The ultimate internal multi-taskers of the world's future
As powerfully unparalleled
And beautiful as supernumerary rainbows
They are not disabled ...
It just means that they are differently-abled...

~ Jamie Bond aka Unmuted Ink

an Autism Awareness Anthology

Superior Hero

THE FANTASTIC FOUR HAS GAINED ONE MORE
ABLE TO TOUCH ANY HEART IN A SINGLE SOUND
I........AM..........JUDE
My super-power is
I have Autism....
But, I snatched out the "U", replaced it with an "R"
Because, my art is, I'm gifted
Lifting my grades past those with no gifts and still
Remain social with all other children
No counselor ,but mommy, she guides me she's the Best of my teachers
The Greatest Mommy in the world as she cheers from the bleachers
No different than any other kid maybe, only, the way that I see things
But that's just like having a broad imagination
So by no stretch am I weakling
Take time to get to know me, open your eyes learn to see more
My name is Jude
I AM......A SUPERHERO!!!!

~Quise "The Notebook" Williams

Different Isn't Bad

Sometimes things just don't make sense,
Why is it easier for my brother to clean his room,
Mom tells me to,
I become confused,
She loves me,
She says different isn't bad,
So she goes step by step,
Not that I am stupid or inept,
Actually my I.Q. Is well above average,
127 is my number since kindergarten too,
I know my colors red, white, and blue,
People say things because I am colorblind too,
Music makes more sense to me,
It quiets what is going on above,
Drawing was my first passion and love,
I have drawn for musicians and the military too,
See different isn't bad and I am only 14,
People think I am disrespectful and rude,
Just because I don't make eye contact,
It doesn't mean I am not listening to you,
Please make my cheeseburger with ketchup on top,
If it isn't up there and a pickle too,
I am sorry but I will give the burger to you,
Momma say different isn't bad,
She helps me embrace it,
She even taught me to talk to people,
See, I use to get mad,
It wasn't that I picked the fight,
I was like Spiderman,
I wouldn't let the bully pick on you,
One time my temper got the best,

an Autism Awareness Anthology

I picked up one boy,
Held him a foot off the ground,
By nothing but my hand on his chest,
I didn't like the feeling,
I didn't know what to do,
But heard mom talking about a counselor,
The lady listened to her,
It made her feel better too,
So I asked to get help,
I didn't like the anger inside,
Since then, I have not been as frustrated,
Or even in a real fight,
I guess at fourteen it is a tough time too,
It doesn't help I tower people at 6'2,
But momma said different isn't bad,
She lets me talk to her about anything,
Even if it might make her mad,
She loves and listens,
Claps louder than most when playing my sax,
She helps me shine it until it glistens,
She has helped me by letting me play loud,
She is the standing ovation that starts the crowd,
So even though I struggle with cleaning my room,
Struggle with what you think are easy things to do,
I am not mad,
Because momma said being different isn't bad...

JRC 12/15/2012 ~Starr Poetress

WELL STACKED

Im a mystery

mystery

mystery

I know you don't understand

understand

understand

and neither do I

I

I

its a miscommunication

a misunderstanding

a glitch

glitch

glitch

like your computer

computer

computer

or your toaster

toaster

toaster

toasting really dark and crispy

crispy

crispy

on the really light setting

setting

setting

or the cable getting news

news

news instead of sports

sports

sports

but that's okay . . . the doctor says I

can still live a normal life

life

life . . .

I'm not different, just . . .

well stacked

stacked

stacked that's all.

~ stuartirvingmarshall

Enigma

Close your eyes and imagine...
Imagine all children being the same
No difference or change, Im talking, same brain
Microchip embedded like, artificial intellegence
Not one any different than the other, I mean, no precedence
Now, open your eyes...
Listen to the voices, the laughter
Different expressions, expressing what they're feeling at that
Very...moment
The looks on their faces and in their eyes
The innocense of the children with no disguise
Now...
Envision your vision as two camera lenses
Able to capture still pixels
Develop and flash-drive save into your memory all in the same instance
Imagine...
Enhanced hearing
Pin-drop precision, sharp as blue-ray, mind spinning like the disk in fast-forward
Without a nucleus...
Volume either mute or extended.
Being able to reminisce without thinking back
Pause button removed
Senses on play, continuously like a Poet with no sense of writer's block
Unintentionally blocking out everything that doesnt belong
Mental auto-correct...
Alt, space, delete

Not starting over but, to refresh
To only continue from where you left off
Attention spanning on spaces and times that, has yet to come
Capable of capturing, that to the superficial and stereotypical is known as normal
Normally diagnosed as a mis-diagnosis to 1 in every 88 children in the U.S
An overly-educated guess of those who have Autism suffer
But, to suffer from Autism is, not to suffer from anything
Its only to establish the super-powers that you were Blessed with
Taking your place
Pacing on
Whatever color your cape
And take flight

~ Quise 'The Notebook' Williams

A Letter to Travon

Twenty nine years ago you entered my life
And what a bundle of joy you were
A teen mother, I had to catch on fast
You were growing
So fast
You babbled just as babies do
But as time went on there was something new
Something different
Something special
You are
 Special
A special young man
With a love for the drums
The keys
And for music altogether
Your love for food is special too
It's the highlight of your day
Pizza, Chicken, Pasta, Greens
Cabbage, Potatoes, and lots of other things
You can be stubborn at times
And insist on having things your way
Still your demeanor is always cool
Mr. Cool, Calm and Collected
That's who you are
And even though you're autistic
To me, you are a star
My star
A star that's not enticed by the streets

an Autism Awareness Anthology

Doing things that could land you in jail
Or making baby after baby
Having lots of stories to tell
Sometimes my patience grows thin
And I need to get away
That's when our support system
Comes to save the day
Tamatha, Jeanette, Bernice and Shirley
Are just to name a few
So many beautiful spirits
Who take good care of you
Please know that you are loved
Today and always

~ Jacqueline Thomas Rome

PUZZLED ~ When the Pieces don't see to Fit

Beautiful Mind

They always told me you were slow
Can't get right
That your mind
Did not work like ours
They teased you
But you never defended yourself
Instead
You took it out
Upon the ivory keys in the in the choir room
As I passed by the melody beckoned me
Like a moth to a flame
To find you at it's source
Creating something breathtaking
I said to myself there's no way he can be slow
The teacher
Seeing shock painted on my face
Told me all anyone needs to bloom is love
No matter how long it may take
I realized in that moment
His mind didn't work like the rest
It didn't operate in the ignorance ours did
Spending our time trying to figure out what box to put you in
So I sat with him
Apologizing for everything
And he continued to play for me
Now I know that no matter what they called him
No matter where he may have fell in the spectrum
His mind
Was synoptic
With his music
Beautiful

~Lion Heart

Misunderstood

I am silent
I am barricaded
Between the four walls of my own mind
I am caged
Trying to find a better way
I want to be heard
Yet, I am so
Misunderstood...
I am sheltered
I am confined
I want to be known
But, fear knowing the world
I want to know sounds
I want to be free
But, I fear what can't be seen
I want friends
But, I am looked at differently...
I appreciate the little things
The heat created from the sun of my skin
How the leaves change colors
And fall differently
How snowflakes have strange patterns
As they finally fall
Or how when its warm
Snow turns into water
And how rain forms puddles
As it accumulates in small spaces
I Love to splash
Yet, I am so
Misunderstood...
I am a prisoner in my own body
In my own mind

PUZZLED ~ When the Pieces don't see to Fit

Brilliant in other's eyes
I have a distant stare
People think that I don't care
I can't stand loud noises
And places with acoustic spaces
These sounds..
Place my hands to my ears
And brings me to my knees
I am an outcast
An outsider
A visionary in my own mind
I will stand strong
Cause, people like Thomas Edison
And Albert Einstein
Were viewed just like me
So, I look up at the sky
And understand that I'm one of a kind
No need to hide
My uniqueness is all I have
Wish people could see past my exterior
See me for more than an empty vessel
I can be more than who I am
I wish people could know me
But, right now...
I am so
Misunderstood.

~ Planted Daisies

an Autism Awareness Anthology

The Heart Of My Heart

My emotions were mirrored in his eyes
for a moment I captured
all the joy I had ever dreamed
from his first smile
I could feel my love surrendering to everything
to be taken by this gift
moved by this thought a heart like mine
breathing life
I speak of the giving
the sharing of this spirit brought me to this understanding
to be the beautiful things love should be
this wanting unlike any other
to have these feelings
when every sound becomes the words
from the beat of my heart, this day and forever
I will always love you

~ Samuel Rain Benjamin

PUZZLED ~ When the Pieces don't see to Fit

an Autism Awareness Anthology

5 LBS 14 OZ

Depressed & Stressed yet I am Blessed
Let me weave you a web, I'm a clever seamstress
I need to address, or rather, confess what's suppressed & pressed way down deep in my chest
And I could care less who knows
As the time goes the more it really shows, I am hurting inside
As much as I try to fight it and hide it, I can't right it, I've tried it, so let me write it
March 22nd, 2004 my life changed forever
I had a little one on the way for me to adore
God said it was time for me to explore
Motherhood
I never knew I ever could, love so hard
It came natural to me, it was in my cards
Through the struggle, the pain and the strain
I got her here, and nothing has been the same
She is my picture, I am her frame
She is my spirit, I gave her, her name
And in my heart forever, she will remain
I hold back my tears now, let me refrain
I'm taking you through my journey, sit back, enjoy the ride, you're on my train
The first time I looked into her eyes, I was mesmerized
She had my mind in a trance, I was hypnotized
My heart did a dance when I heard her first cries
It was real to me then, she was really alive
Weighin' in at a mere five
5 LBS, 14 OZS
I'm holding back the tears as I pronounce this:
My little princess, as God is my witness

PUZZLED ~ When the Pieces don't see to Fit

There is apart of my soul that will never forgive this:
At 3 years old, she was diagnosed with autism
My soul COLLASPED into a PRiSON
I was lost in myself, I forgot my vision
I had no breath left to breathe, it was a sad condition, with no ways to set provisions
Then Came Transition\
Which was hard on me at first
Autism transpired into my escapism
I became a dead prism
Darkness took hold of me that first year, fearing the light I did not go near her
But it was fear that got me here
Let me draw back & make this clear
Even now I have my fears
And my God, O my God, I have cried so many tears throughout these past 3 years
Nothing inside is like the exterior appears~ My soul LEERS
Feeling malicious
Everyone around me at some points have been fake, just fictitious
So I strike those foes down with verses so vicious
And revenge is sweet, trust me, it tastes delicious
But not as delicious as forgiveness
Forgiveness of Self
Stowing anger away; buried that book deep in my shelf
And I never want to read it again
Please miss me with the B.S. you are NOT my friend
Anger, there's no need to pretend, you're a sin.
Let's begin so we can mend and then come to the end
She's my kin, My daughter
And if someone tries to hurt her, it is them who I will slaughter

an Autism Awareness Anthology

Like the air i breathe she has become my living water and that's why I'm harder...
I am stronger today than I was yesterday
And my tomorrow's are not full of sorrows nor joy borrowed
My joy will be real
You just don't understand how I feel, it's surreal
I went to the Lord's courts and made my appeals
Then he sentenced my heart to heal
It's a sealed deal, for real
So when I look at this mess, this ordeal
I have no reason to hide nor conceal
Despite the fact that it is not ideal
I still have a heart full of zeal
So I kneel
And Pray, thanking the Lord for this day
I will not be dismayed
I will walk in His shade
For this is the day that the Lord has made
And I will rejoice, even though I was not given a choice
The Lord still gave me a voice
And I am... Speaking

~ Ashley Diaz McDaniel * The Lyrical Gymnast

You Are Beautiful
(Dedicated to Special Needs Children)

So people look at you strange..

Oh that poor child..

Oh what their parent must go through..

But you are better than them,

Cause you do the best you can do..

So you walked a little late?

So your speech is delayed?

So maybe you are a little behind..

But a smile like yours is hard to find..

Your inner beauty..

Through your smile..

Brings inspiration..

Brings happiness to me..

You are gods gift to the world..

So ease your worried mind..

So you are special needs..

What difference does that really make?

You.. are a precious angel.

And the purity in you is something we all seek to find..

So,

You are different..

Well...

Arent we all..

But at least you do the best you can..

Your smile brings happiness to my day..

Your happiness always takes my worries away..

You alwys remind me of the lost innocence in me..

You always make me amazed by your purity..

You are gods gift to the world..

never let anyone tell you you are not,,

You remind us all of how we should be..

You always bring a smile that sets my heart free..

You are an angel on earth..

You are gods gift to the world..

You..

Are beautiful..

My special needs child..

~ Patrick Read

Little Window

My love

I understand that you do not want to play

Again today

And it is okay

So I will just watch you and wish that I could hold you

closer

Longer

Or even at all

Just if I could comfort you when you fall

But I know deep down inside that it is something bigger

than mommy's wants

It is more the nature of your needs

If I could be sure that you know it, even though you do not

show it

I am here

When I look into your little eyes I adore you, my child

Even though I have never ever seen your precious lips

smile

Or I have never heard the sound of your sweet voice

Your presence in my life gives me no other choice

Than to love and love and love you

You are my world even though I may not be in yours

I am here

Watching you grow and explore without me

I will not question my blessing in disguise

My bundle of joy that brings me delight and surprise

Our routine will continue tomorrow and the next day and the one after that

For the rest of our lives together in fact

My love

So sleep well and sleep tight

I will meet you tomorrow

On the other side of your eyes

~ Krystal Davis "Lypstyk"

PUZZLED ~ When the Pieces don't see to Fit

Your Name is Not Autistic

Reminiscing...a collage of memories....
I'm remembering the day you were born, as perfect as can be
A wondrous Blessing to our Family
A Gift to He and Me

That smile, your first steps
I'll never forget,
As I realized those steps would symbolize
The many steps you'd take through Life

Your curiosities grew vigorously
You were always getting into this and that
And though you attempted to communicate rigorously
The words wouldn't come then, No not yet...

I cried so many tears,
Had so many fears
God what could I have done wrong?
Searching my soul for answers, He said to be strong.

Though no chatter, I enjoyed the sounds of your laughter,
By your mind I was constantly Amazed,
The things you could do at such a young age,
How without saying a word you could spell your name.

You'd cling to me
Tugs and hums meant "Mommy sing to me"
I'd sing the Go-To-Sleep song...
The way you'd pull my hand across your chest to say
"Don't go yet...stay long"

PUZZLED ~ When the Pieces don't see to Fit

And that day would finally come
No more jargon,
Smiling with few a words along, you said
"Arms, legs, head…"
Yes baby… arms, legs, head…
That's what you said

Through tears I thanked God again and again
Knowing for you, this was just the beginning…

Birthdays, Graduations,
Going from situation to situation
Experiencing new things-
Bike rides, skates parks, and soaring in swings

Seeming to soar and excel in everything you do
But socialization was always the hardest part for you.
And though you'd try, frustrations made you cry
We'd always tell you…baby it's alright,
It will come some time…

And Time just went
As here you are practically a man
Now aware, you don't understand-
Why people don't understand all of the demands
This thing has on your mental

You wish patience was longer and the world was more gentle,
Less complex in fact even though your mind's not that simple
Sometimes it's too much; living with this is just too tough
You say you just can't and you want to give up…

Listen...Your Name is Not Autistic
It's an attribute of God, meaning Master
So I know You will Master This!

You are Brilliant, though different
Your Uniqueness is a Gift, it's Your Strength
Though at times you may think it makes you weak
...I just wish you could see what I see...

When I look at you I don't see a disability
Though it often leers at me-
Through stubbornness, meltdowns and tantrum-fits

I do attempt,
To see right to your soul
The true you that is what I behold
That child I use to hold, that boy so brave and bold

Filled with such determination and hope
Climbing on top of table tops to look back to see how far he'd gone
"Boy get down before you fall..." Though with hope you never failed
Through my hope you never will, because within you I see a strong will
A might to build faith upon the highest hill-
Mountain tops! So stand a-top and look again at how far you Got!

Yes you've made it this far
So Always, Always be Proud of Who You Are
Your Name is Not Autistic...
Though different, still...
YOU-ARE-BRIL-LIANT...

~ Linda Terrell

PUZZLED ~ When the Pieces don't see to Fit

an Autism Awareness Anthology

A Mother's Piece

Living in a city called Baltimore
Met a few friends and saw them endure
The birth of their sons and daughters
Filled with the hopes and dreams their parent taught us
But yet interesting how fate plays it's hand
Hard to figure out and understand
This baby was born perfect you see
But around eighteen months something escaped me
Couldn't figure out why I no longer heard the sound
Of babbling words and along with playing toys around
Trying to figure out what is his or her fate
A mother contends, rewinds trying to figure out the mistake
Was is something about the pregnancy, she prays for a clue
Trying to figure out what took over her baby like a Coue
But yet she can't undue what has already been done
Now time seek help from the doctors, and now it has begun
They poke, they prod, they ask a ton of questions
About diet, environments searching
for something to measure
But immeasurable disappointments
come over and over again
Mom, is now isolated no one to depend
They no longer come over to visit the new baby
Now they talk behind her back about how it's so crazy
A toddler very young should be talking at best
Now all this mom needs is good nights rest
Restless baby this child has become, sleepless nights
Knock down fights, the plight has just begun...
Doctors and specialist, special diets,
trying to find the trigger

PUZZLED ~ When the Pieces don't see to Fit

Of how this child has grown into something
they are trying to figure
Socially incomplete and unable
to compete in a cold cruel world
She seeks support, schools, library
and psychological reports as they all unfurl..
Leaving her to wonder what
will become of my son or daughter,
How will they grow up and will they be smarter
Coping mechanisms are amazing and some do succeed
But many are left at the school house
steps waiting to proceed
This disability bites hard
and we are just trying to find the right muzzle
As we move to work with the child with Autism
find the missing piece to the puzzle…

~Isolda McClelland "Soul"

On The Inside

Locked away in the rooms of your mind
I know you're in there.
I see flashes of you dance across your face
Even if you cant look my way
I watch in awe of your existence.
My holding you may seem restrictive
I'm sorry.
I only wish to take the confusion away
I want to understand.
In the small tatters of torn yesterdays
I imagined a perfect world
Where we could talk and laugh
Conversations would be unending
But now I struggle to see what you're saying
When the air is still
My love for you is a promise
A vow held without account
Of return
You are beautiful in your ways
How could I not want you to be here?
Living life on the inside.
I bet you dance when I'm away
And sing when I'm gone
Your voice is that gold
at the end of the rainbow
Your smile, the apple of my eye
I hold you in my heart.
For always...
Even if the key is not found.

~CarLa "SugaBrown" Howard-Daniels

Peculiar Puzzle

I know you view my condition as a hindrance.
I see it as having a unique vision,
placing life's lines in my own position.
My speech carries an eccentric rhythm,
my thoughts travel on a scenic pattern.
What I hear and what you hear
occupy perpendicular wavelengths.
Don't mock me because I'm different.

It's possible I won't remember your name;
however, I can possess a more potent abstract memory.
You see, the quadratic equation
of my existence is more exponential than
your parenthetical prejudice and
multiplied misconception of who I am.
The latent layers of me will enlighten thee,
once you appreciate the genuine smile on my face.

My mental pieces form a vibrant puzzle.
To you it may seem jumbled,
but to me it's picture perfect.
I'll admit that I can be trouble,
nonetheless, my heart remains harmless.
I never asked to be born this way.
God made me from birth, who I am today

Here's a little spectrum about me
I...
Actualize unique areas of my potential.
Utilize the life given to me to my best ability.
Test my limits and the limits of others.
Impact the lives of those around me with humility.
Sync my contact with the world peculiarly.
Motivate others unlike me to appreciate their complete cognitive freedom.

I am Autistic if you have not figured it out.
So, what do you think of me now?

~Soul Q

To Hold You My Child

My Child,

Encamped inside my spirit

Anticipating the moments

I crave your whispers of calling me Mommy

And tender butterfly kisses

Navigating spirals of tolerance

I strive so vigorously and delicately

Patiently waiting to live in your loving

Embrace if only for a moment!

I pray ...

For tomorrow, is yet another day

We will strive together

Blessed in our Journey

Me, You, Mommy and I

~ Carlene Beverly

10 Perfect Fingers & 10 Perfect Toes

10 perfect fingers & 10 perfect toes you watch as your little blessing grows

Playing and cooing happiness shows

But it's as if all of a sudden time froze

Or got thrown in reverse

And by the age of three you begin to see a slowdown developmentally

A kind of regression

Not sure of what to do you find yourself stressin wondering how you prepare for this curve ball life has thrown

How could you have known

Denial is your first reaction

Not my child this just can't be

You see I did everything right

Took my vitamins got my check ups

counted 10 perfect fingers and 10 perfect toes, two ears, two eyes, and a perfect little nose

But you can't dismiss the fact that something's amiss

Communication's a struggle

At times turn to tantrums and rages

Shying from affection just one of many characteristics in the autism spectrum

PUZZLED ~ When the Pieces don't see to Fit

Can't imagine your child not wanting your affection

Not having that connection

That bonds mother and child

Diagnosis range from severe to mild

him and his Aspergers or her with her Rhett's

The doctor gives results after a battery of tests

You could be crying out why you

But instead you do what must be done

No praise no applause

Long nights turn to day

Trying to learn all you can

Try to understand

Formulate a plan to help

To raise awareness

To the fact that 1 in 54 boys and 1 in 252 girls are diagnosed

But it doesn't affect us til it hits home

You'd do the same for those 10 perfect little fingers and 10 perfect little toes

~ Blaque Diamond

an Autism Awareness Anthology

Brother

My sister left me today

All alone in this little room

Mom says I must stay

So she can keep me safe

And I am sometimes

I just can't make her understand

That I need my sister

To play under this tent

She will hold my hand

When the noise is too loud

And tell me secrets

When the noise is too quiet

Mommy, mommy, mommy

I want her mommy

Because she has to go

To normal school and I close

My eyes against sunlight

When it gets too close

Then I must take

My medicine, red, blue, yellow

Counting them all every day

And I want my sister

To come and stay forever

PUZZLED ~ When the Pieces don't see to Fit

I sleep with my eyes open
And walk with my eyes closed
I want sugar candy now
But daddy says no
So when he is sleep
I throw away his socks
So he can't leave the house
Either, never, no, no, no
But somehow he still
Will leave for work in the snow
My sister has a birthday

I have a book I read
When no one is looking
It says my sister was born
On a Wednesday in the afternoon
I want to know if the sun
Was shining on Wednesdays
Cause it hurts the baby's eyes
And I want my sister to come
Because she has the answers
My friend at school says
His sister is a bitch and whore
My sister will know what it is

an Autism Awareness Anthology

I looked for my sister
At the church in the country
She wasn't with the other
Sister-sisters and sister-cousins
My grandmother is dead
My aunt says she is no longer here
My sister isn't here either
I tried to ask where she was
But they just said "shhh"
I wanted to cry but I kicked
At the pew in front of me
My sister is not here
I hope my sister
Is not dead too

~ Gail Weston Shazor

Autism Life

People with autism can be
a little autistic or very autistic.
Thus, it is possible to be bright, verbal,
and autistic as well as mentally retarded,
non-verbal and autistic.
A disorder that includes such a broad range
of symptoms is often called a spectrum disorder;
hence the term "autism spectrum disorder."
The most significant shared symptom is difficulty
with social communication
(eye contact, conversation,
taking another's perspective, etc.).
imagine a world that was difficult to be social
to enjoy friendships as you do now
to communicate in the ways you are used to
like being in a glass cage,
you can see and hear and feel everyone
yet they cannot touch you,
they cannot connect with you
how heartbreaking that must be
what a difficult road to travel down life's path
yet they accomplish their goals in life
love shines from their beings
happiness is there way
God bless these souls

~ Mimi T. Davis

an Autism Awareness Anthology

Hush Little Baby

Hush, little baby, don't say a word
Daddy's gonn-a buy you a mocking-bird
And if that Mocking bird don't...sing

When people ask me,
I tell them that son's favorite word
Is oooooooooooohhhhhhhhhhhh!

See, my son is autistic
And he doesn't talk
But last night I had a dream
That my son spoke to me.

And, when I woke up,
I cried.
Never thought that
I could be denied
The simple pleasure of
Words heard from the mouth
Of my child!
But that seems to be
The reality of the situation.

Feeling, frustration.
Mad at the world;
Hell, mad at God!
Hard to bare but there
Is a deafening silence
In my house
Even when conversation
Is in full bloom

PUZZLED ~ When the Pieces don't see to Fit

Because, his words are missing.
And, as the cloud of autism looms
Over my head like guillotines
Ready to drop, all I can do
Is hope that the symptoms will stop

And it's funny,
Because I'm supposed to be
That guy that you come to
With your problems;
But who do I talk to,
About the son who can't talk to me?
Can't, tell me that he's hungry
That, he wants to play.
Hold it in everyday,
But sometimes I wanna lash out!
Hit walls! Throw things until
I throw my back out! But,
That woudn't do me any good, No.

See, not much is understood about autism
But I do know this;
The shit hurts, like curse the heavens!
And bring the hearse,
Because when they told me that my son And I
Couldn't converse, I was ready to die.
Felt like I was empty inside like I had no soul
Heart felt so cold and open,
But forget about females because
This is heartbreak of a different kind.

I mean I've wanted to be dad
Since the one I had
Decided he had better things to do
And so, while it's true

That he is the cutest little
Half-black, half-jew you've
Ever seen, behind the scenes,
Things aren't what they seem.

And so last night in that dream;
I dreamt that he could speak,
I dream that he could speak,
Just that, I was deaf to his cries
That he, was reaching for me
But I couldn't see him with these eyes.

And it's so hopelessly ironic
That I'm supposedly so good with words
But the one person I want to reach
I can't
So when I see these fucked up fathers out here
I'm quick to rant
And rave
I mean, how dare you behave in any manner
Other than absolute obsession
Over your health child

Like, the other day...
My friend, said that if his son was gay;
He would disOWN him.
Said he "personally had no problem with gays
But there was no ways their ways would
Be the ways of his boy"

I told him "that's fucked up"
That he wouldn't love his own child
Uncondtionally. He said, "Ok,
What would you do if your son was gay?"

PUZZLED ~ When the Pieces don't see to Fit

I said "Ray, if tomorrow after my son's day
At school, as I removed his shoes
He used his first words to tell me
He had a crush on a boy...

...I would do three things.
One; I would pinch myself,
For fear that I was once again merely dreaming.
Two, I would hold him, so tightly he'd have to bite me
To remove himself from my grip, and
Three, I would ask him what the kid's name was
Because I know there are far worse things can happen
To your child then you not agreeing with his or her sexual preference.

Sometimes, I wonder if when he sleeps, he dreams...
Of a father who isnt bothered by the fact he can't speak
Who, doesnt think it fair to compare him to other kids his age
Who understands that love is not expressed in words but in smiles
And hands held tightly on summer sunday afternoons

Jasaant you don't to say a fucking word,
Daddy's gonna talk loud enough for the both of us,
And I promise, won't NOBODY shut me up!

~ David Colvert

an Autism Awareness Anthology

On the Word "Autistic"

This ain't chalk-dust slur-ghost
snaking from blacktop belly of playground;
not my shiniest marble snatched
by bully-claws.
There is no reclamation here.
This is not about ownership.

Autism doesn't sit on my back fence
flapping flightless arms like naked wings.
Autism doesn't lurk at the end of the bar in a sleazy suit
slipping stutters and tics into my drink when I'm not
looking.
Autism doesn't follow me around like a pet;
the awkward in my gair is not leash-drag or sidestep.
Autism doesn't hang from the shelf of my ribs
like a tumor to be excised,
to bring me back to normal.
I have no normal to go back to.

I was an easy, happy baby
who burbled perfect pitch from my crib
then I was a two-year-old dropped in the maze
of the honeycomb linoleum pattern.
I was a five-year-old spinning in circles
instead of watching cartoons.
I was a nine-year-old on the edge of the kickball field
sifting red dust between my fingers while the ball sailed
past me.
I was a teenager learning social graces
as a second language.

PUZZLED ~ When the Pieces don't see to Fit

I was an adult teaching people like me
how to use our neighbors as mirrors
to navigate a world we were born without a map to.
I am damn good at it
and this is the only normal I've ever been.

People have cancer.
People have lupus.
People have polio.
Remove these things, or look beyond them
and the person who carries them remains the same.
There is no autism without autistic people.
Remove it,
and you snip the thin silver wire,
like the singular hair that sprouted at my temple after my last birthday,
that runs mercurial through the lobes of my brain,
plugs into the lens through which I see the world.
You turn me into someone else.

It's this same different wiring that makes it make sense to us
to say that calling us autistic people is still putting people first.
I am not a person with autism.
I would not be the same person without it.
I am not here to take back this word, "autistic."
You can't take back something
that has been inside you the whole time.

Gabe Moses

This Gifted Child

When I was two . . .
you noticed something different
not less than or equal to.

Not like my brothers and sisters
who interacted well
in the park with others
playing tag . . .
or racing passed me.

You just couldn't see . . .
by the way that I rocked to and fro;
seemingly staring into space
that I was on stage with
a full orchestra in tow.

What you did not know
is that I was conducting
symphonies in my head
all composed by me.

As you know
I did grow
through the traumas
and dramas
both on and off stage.

This Gifted Child now
a gifted man . . .
and a well – known Composer.

~ Janet P. Caldwell

being possible

i saw the colors
they were so bright and clear
dancing in my visions
but you could not see them could you
so i painted them just for you
so that you could feel them
as i do

i heard the music
the Choir of Angels Sang for me
but you did not hear them did you
so i sat at the Piano
the Harp
the Guitar
and i played them
just for you

there are many things i see
i hear
i feel
that are quite real
that i bring to the world
just for you
but you do not always have time

to look at me
see me
do you

i may be different
as seen through your eyes
but your God
my God
loves me to
in a very special way

he sent me here
to help you find your way
this day
by showing you the things
you can not see
can not hear
can not imagine
being possible

william s. peters, sr.

PUZZLED ~ When the Pieces don't see to Fit

An Open Letter to My Sun

Sun,

There have been many days that I've taken pen to pad trying to form the words to write something…anything, about you…for you, but the words that came never seemed to be enough. And even now as I sit here, I'm not sure if these words will suffice. How do you explain to a child that you were LIFE sparked in the darkness of a mourning womb, a dream planted in depressed soil, how do I make you understand? You were the greatest gift any Winter morning could bring, you are my perfectly imperfect piece of a dream. When I look back over your life, I don't remember clouds, the storm or the rain showers that met with the sun to cast the beautiful kaleidoscope of colors in your sky. I only remember that you have always been colored beautiful and that those colors, some more vivid than others, were always present.

I've seen your aura change as your emotions banged around your insides like a bull crashing around in a China Shop making you Red with frustration. When your eyes are the saddest I've ever seen, causing the levees that hold the tears at bay, to break from the weight of Blue. When the volume of your voice box is turned up, there are Yellows and Oranges that vibrate with every word formed and I'd ask you " Hey Jude, why are you talking so loud?" Then I remember the colors and what they mean, the happiness and excitement you feel being able to hear your own voice forming words into sentences, when at one time you could not.

The times when you are tickled Pink and your laughter is contagious, we all find ourselves laughing and we really don't know why. The Purple that puffs out your chest with pride from being an excellent student, holding a top position in your class. There is a bright white, when your eyes stare in wonderment and I see you absorbing everything around you. Making me wish I could trade eyes with you just to see the world the way you do, I can only imagine how spectacular the simplest things we take for granted appear through your eyes. I've always wondered about the Greens, if there are moments that you wished you were more like the other children. Do you even know that there is a difference or if you think they are the abnormal ones?

One day I hope you know that being different is beautiful, just as God blessed me to be the vessel from which you were born, HE made you uniquely you for a reason. On those days when this thing called Autism causes your spirit to sag, leaving the pride in your spine hunched and all I can do is hold you, know that I would burden my back bone for you. If I could take it from you and carry it, I would for as long as you needed. I know sometimes this life feels like free falling through the sky, but I'm not concerned about the fall because I know with this gift you can become anything you want. Become Icarus fashion your own wings, built with perseverance and strength with no worries of wings made of melting wax.

You're much smarter than that and you out shine any Sun hung in the sky. You...my perfectly imperfect piece of a dream, are the closest thing to magic I have ever experienced. When you are older I hope you read this and understand that those moments of frustration you may have witnessed or the tears I tried to hide were just my way of releasing my colors. That it in no way was a direct reflection of you, know that I am imperfect, but trying to be the most perfect Mom for you. And yes Sun we all have colors they just show themselves differently, your colors are just bold and bright always remember that. I am grateful, humbled, proud and filled with Love, it is an absolute honor being your mom.

I Love You to Life,

Mommy

~Yvette

PUZZLED ~ When the Pieces don't see to Fit

PICTURES
+
GRAPHICS

an Autism Awareness Anthology

"If they can't learn the way we teach,
we teach the way they learn"
~O. Ivar Lovaas

> 'Art can permeate
> the very deepest part of us,
> where no words exist.'
> Eileen Miller
> The Girl Who Spoke with Pictures:
> Autism Through Art

"You have to be the bravest person in the world to go out every day, being yourself when no one likes who you are."
~Matthew Dicks, Memoirs of an Imaginary Friend

PUZZLED ~ When the Pieces don't see to Fit

"The worst thing you can do is nothing."
~Temple Grandin

an Autism Awareness Anthology

"I may not make eye contact but at least I don't stare"
~unknown

PUZZLED ~ When the Pieces don't see to Fit

"Autism:
Where the 'randomness of life'
collides and clashes with an individual's
need for the sameness"
~Eileen Miller,
The Girl Who Spoke with Pictures:
Autism Through Art

"I like nonsense, it wakes up the brain cells.
Fantasy is a necessary ingredient in living,
It's a way of looking at life through the wrong end of a telescope.
Which is what I do. And that enables you to laugh at life's realities."
- Dr Seus

an Autism Awareness Anthology

PUZZLED ~ When the Pieces don't see to Fit

"He is his own snowflake...
no two are the same"
~Aoise Williams

an Autism Awareness Anthology

"Her beautiful mind
Revealed itself through
Artisitc and Intellectual
Blessings that she
Embodied...
Such class this girl has...
Way beyond a 7 year old's
Interpretation of
The world...
A not so innocent world
She came to ultimately know...
Fundamentally different from
The meticulously framed
Stage she'd call
'Maya's show'....." ~Isis Sun,
　excerpt from poem entitled "Sunshine"

PUZZLED ~ When the Pieces don't see to Fit

an Autism Awareness Anthology

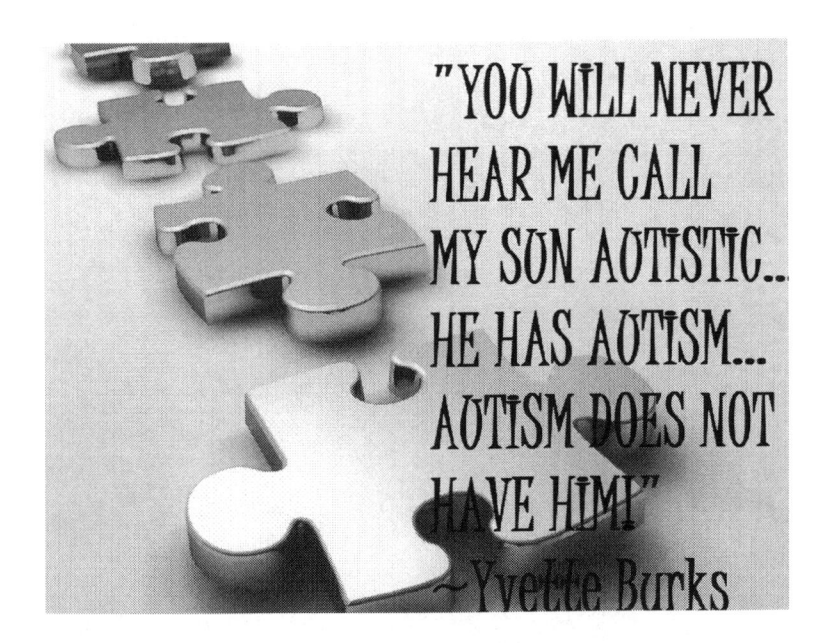

"YOU WILL NEVER HEAR ME CALL MY SON AUTISTIC... HE HAS AUTISM... AUTISM DOES NOT HAVE HIM!"
~Yvette Burks

PUZZLED ~ When the Pieces don't see to Fit

~ EPILOGUE ~

in Other Words...

When Jude was about two years old, we noticed that he had not met his speech and language milestones. Our initial thought was that the chronic ear infections he endured as an infant affected his hearing causing a developmental delay in his speech. We immediately had his hearing tested, passing those tests we moved on to speech evaluation. He was then diagnosed as having a speech delay and soon after that he began speech therapy, but something still didn't register and as a Mother you just know when something is not quite right with your child.

Jude also exhibited issues with Sensory perception; he didn't like his hands wet and at every meal he would smell his food before tasting it. From then on the winding road to the final diagnosis of AUTISM became a long three year journey. Most of the precursors that doctors look for he did not exhibit, after a 1st, 2nd and 3rd opinion and a full team diagnostic evaluation, in December of 2011 Jude was diagnosed as having Autism Spectrum Disorder. Because he is so highly functioning, his ASD presented itself on the milder end of the spectrum.

During my research and experience, I've found that my travel down this road was not as treacherous as some families who deal with the more severe end of the spectrum. Imagine waking one day to find your happy healthy child disappearing into him or herself or having a child that cannot speak. Can you imagine how devastating it would be for all the hopes and dreams you had for your child to be shattered with one word...AUTISM. As with any setback there is always hope and the previous dreams, become dreams deferred morphing into new dreamscapes.

The rate of incidence of children being diagnosed is rising from 1 in 88 in March of 2012 to the frightening estimation of 1 in 9 by the year 2022. Although there have been many theories, the cause of Autism is still unknown. With no explanations for this mysterious disorder there have been no cures to date only treatment options.

There are many obstacles that we as families affected with ASD have to overcome like government funding, insurance coverage and education reform. Acceptance, awareness and compassion from our respective communities is a definite start.

I hope that by purchasing and reading this book, it has sparked an interest to want to learn more. To at least open dialogue with others and find compassion for the children and families affected, in turn encouraging you to get involved. Autism is seen as an incurable affliction to some, but to others it's seen as a gift, a God connection, whether you believe it to be one or the other get informed.

~Yvette Burks

"Autism: Where the "randomness of life" collides and clashes with an individual's need for the sameness" — Eileen Miller, *The Girl Who Spoke with Pictures: Autism Through Art*

Articles & Information

The following information beyond this point is aimed at elevation our awareness of the many considerations of Autism and how it affects the lives of all the people who are blessed to know someone who has been diagnosed or not.

Please take the time to not only familiarize your self with the information and Resources, but to pass it on to others that they to ay become enlightened about the many aspects that may affect them, their Families and Humanity.

Thank You

Yvette Burks

an Autism Awareness Anthology

What Is Autism?

What Is Autism? What is Autism Spectrum Disorder?

Autism spectrum disorder (ASD) and autism are both general terms for a group of complex disorders of brain development. These disorders are characterized, in varying degrees, by difficulties in social interaction, verbal and nonverbal communication and repetitive behaviors. They include autistic disorder, Rett syndrome, childhood disintegrative disorder, pervasive developmental disorder-not otherwise specified (PDD-NOS) and Asperger syndrome. With the May 2013 publication of the new DSM-5 diagnostic manual, these autism subtypes will be merged into one umbrella diagnosis of ASD.

ASD can be associated with intellectual disability, difficulties in motor coordination and attention and physical health issues such as sleep and gastrointestinal disturbances. Some persons with ASD excel in visual skills, music, math and art.

Autism appears to have its roots in very early brain development. However, the most obvious signs of autism and symptoms of autism tend to emerge between 2 and 3 years of age. Autism Speaks continues to fund research on effective methods for earlier diagnosis, as early intervention with proven behavioral therapies can improve outcomes. Increasing autism awareness is a key aspect of this work and one in which our families and volunteers play an invaluable role. Learn more ...

How Common Is Autism?

Autism statistics from the U.S. Centers for Disease Control and Prevention (CDC) identify around 1 in 88 American children as on the autism spectrum–a ten-fold increase in prevalence in 40 years. Careful research shows that this increase is only partly explained by improved diagnosis and awareness. Studies also show that autism is four to five times more common among boys than girls. An estimated 1 out of 54 boys and 1 in 252 girls are diagnosed with autism in the United States.

By way of comparison, more children are diagnosed with autism each year than with juvenile diabetes, AIDS or cancer, combined.* ASD affects over 2 million individuals in the U.S. and tens of millions worldwide. Moreover, government autism statistics suggest that prevalence rates have increased 10 to 17 percent annually in recent years. There is no established explanation for this continuing increase, although improved diagnosis and environmental influences are two reasons often considered. Learn more ...

What Causes Autism?

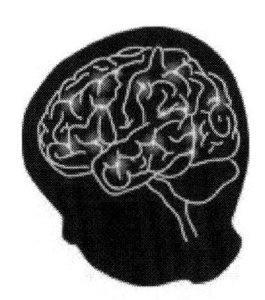

Not long ago, the answer to this question would have been "we have no idea." Research is now delivering the answers. First and foremost, we now know that there is no one cause of autism just as there is no one type of autism. Over the last five years, scientists have identified a number of rare gene changes, or mutations, associated with autism. A small number of these are sufficient to cause autism by themselves. Most cases of autism, however, appear to be caused by a combination of autism risk genes and environmental factors influencing early brain development.

In the presence of a genetic predisposition to autism, a number of nongenetic, or "environmental," stresses appear to further increase a child's risk. The clearest evidence of these autism risk factors involves events before and during birth. They include advanced parental age at time of conception (both mom and dad), maternal illness during pregnancy and certain difficulties during birth, particularly those involving periods of oxygen deprivation to the baby's brain. It is important to keep in mind that these factors, by themselves, do not cause autism. Rather, in combination with genetic risk factors, they appear to modestly increase risk.

A growing body of research suggests that a woman can reduce her risk of having a child with autism by taking prenatal vitamins containing folic acid and/or eating a diet rich in folic acid (at least 600 mcg a day) during the months before and after conception.

Increasingly, researchers are looking at the role of the immune system in autism. Autism Speaks is working to increase awareness and investigation of these and other issues, where further research has the potential to improve the lives of those who struggle with autism. Learn more ...

What Does It Mean to Be "On the Spectrum"?

Each individual with autism is unique. Many of those on the autism spectrum have exceptional abilities in visual skills, music and academic skills. About 40 percent have average to above average intellectual abilities. Indeed, many persons on the spectrum take deserved pride in their distinctive abilities and "atypical" ways of viewing the world. Others with autism have significant disability and are unable to live independently. About 25 percent of individuals with ASD are nonverbal but can learn to communicate using other means. Autism Speaks' mission is to improve the lives of all those on the autism spectrum. For some, this means the development and delivery of more effective treatments that can address significant challenges in communication and physical health. For others, it means increasing acceptance, respect and support.

How Is Autism Diagnosed?

Presently, we don't have a medical test that can diagnose autism. Instead, specially trained physicians and psychologists administer autism-specific behavioral evaluations.

Often parents are the first to notice that their child is showing unusual behaviors such as failing to make eye contact, not responding to his or her name or playing with toys in unusual, repetitive ways. For a description of early indicators of autism, see Learn the Signs.

The Modified Checklist of Autism in Toddlers (M-CHAT) is a list of informative questions about your child. The answers can indicate whether he or she should be further evaluated by a specialist such as a developmental pediatrician, neurologist, psychiatrist or psychologist. (Take the M-CHAT here.)

We encourage parents to trust their instincts and find a doctor who will listen and refer their child to appropriate specialists for diagnosis. Unfortunately, doctors unfamiliar with diagnosing autism sometimes dismiss parent concerns, delaying diagnosis and the opportunity for early intervention therapies. Autism Speaks and other autism organizations are working hard to raise awareness of early signs among physicians as well as parents.

From birth to at least 36 months of age, every child should be screened for developmental milestones during routine well visits. When such a screening—or a parent—raises concerns about a child's development, the doctor should refer the child to a specialist in developmental evaluation and early intervention.

These evaluations should include hearing and lead exposure tests as well as an autism-specific screening tool such as the M-CHAT. Among these screening tools are several geared to older children and/or specific autism spectrum disorders. (Also see our pages on What Is Autism?, Asperger Syndrome and PDD-NOS.)

A typical diagnostic evaluation involves a multidisciplinary team of doctors including a pediatrician, psychologist, speech and language pathologist and occupational therapist. Genetic testing may likewise be recommended, as well as screening for related medical issues such as sleep difficulties. This type of comprehensive helps parents understand as much as possible about their child's strengths and needs. (For local and regional centers specializing in the coordinated medical care of children and adolescents with autism, explore our Autism Treatment Network and visit our Resources page)

Sometimes an autism spectrum disorder is diagnosed later in life, often in relation to learning, social or emotional difficulties. As with young children, diagnosis of adolescents and adults involves personal observation and interview by a trained specialist. Often, a diagnosis brings relief to those who have long struggled with difficulties in relating socially while not understanding the source of their difficulties. A diagnosis can also open access to therapies and assistive technologies that can improve function in areas of difficulty and, so, improve overall quality of life. (Learn more about Adult Services here.)

DSM-IV (DSM-4) criteria for a diagnosis of autism

Physicians use the Diagnostic and Statistical Manual (DSM) for Mental Disorders to determine whether a person has an autism spectrum disorder. The latest version of this manual is the DSM-IV. Its criteria for autism include the following:

I. A total of six (or more) items from heading (A), (B) and (C) with at least two from (A) and one each from (B) and (C):

(A) Qualitative impairment in social interaction as manifested by at least two of the following:

Marked impairments in the use of multiple nonverbal behaviors such as eye-to-eye gaze, facial expression, body posture and gestures to regulate social interaction.

Failure to develop peer relationships appropriate to developmental level.

A lack of spontaneous seeking to share enjoyment, interests or achievements with other people, (e.g. a lack of showing, bringing or pointing out objects of interest to other people).

A lack of social or emotional reciprocity.

(B) Qualitative impairments in communication as manifested by at least one of the following:

Delay in or total lack of the development of spoken language (not accompanied by an attempt to compensate through alternative modes of communication such as gesture or mime).

In individuals with adequate speech, marked impairment in the ability to initiate or sustain a conversation with others.

Stereotyped and repetitive use of language or idiosyncratic language.

Lack of varied, spontaneous make-believe play or social imitative play appropriate to developmental level.

(C) Restricted repetitive and stereotyped patterns of behavior, interests and activities as manifested by at least two of the following:

Encompassing preoccupation with one or more stereotyped and restricted patterns of interest that is abnormal either in intensity or focus

Apparently inflexible adherence to specific nonfunctional routines or rituals

Stereotyped and repetitive motor mannerisms (e.g. hand or finger flapping or twisting, or complex whole-body movements)

Persistent preoccupation with parts of objects

II. Delays or abnormal functioning in at least one of the following areas, with onset prior to age 3 years:

(A) Social interaction

(B) Language used in social communication

(C) Symbolic or imaginative play

DSM-V (DSM-5)

The American Psychiatric Association is currently revising the medical definition of autism spectrum disorder in ways that are expected to change its diagnostic characteristics. This change is expected to be finalized by the end of 2012 and put into practice in 2013. For perspective on the proposed changes and what they might mean for you or your loved one, please see a related statement by Autism Speaks Chief Science Officer, Geri Dawson, Ph.D.

For more information and resources, please see our Video Glossary and FAQs and special sections on Symptoms, Learn the Signs, Treatment, Your Child's Rights, Asperger Syndrome and PDD-NOS. We also offer a number of resource-packed tool kits for free download (here and here). They include our 100 Day Kit for families who have a child recently diagnosed with autism. *These resources are made possible through the generous support of our families, volunteers and other donors.*

Symptoms

What Are the Symptoms of Autism?

Autism spectrum disorders (ASD) are characterized by social-interaction difficulties, communication challenges and a tendency to engage in repetitive behaviors. However, symptoms and their severity vary widely across these three core areas. Taken together, they may result in relatively mild challenges for someone on the high functioning end of the autism spectrum. For others, symptoms may be more severe, as when repetitive behaviors and lack of spoken language interfere with everyday life.

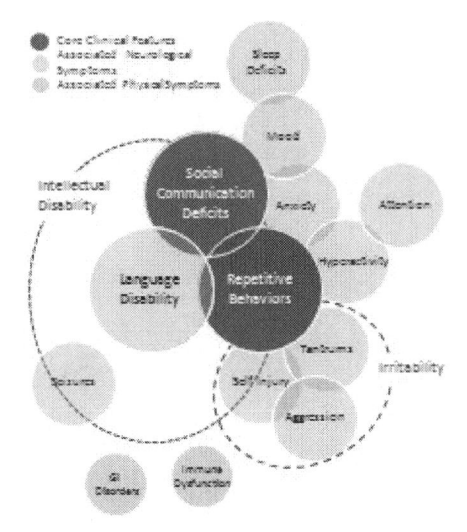

As illustrated by the graph on the left, the basic symptoms of autism are often accompanied other medical conditions and challenges. These, too, can vary widely in severity.

While autism is usually a life-long condition, all children and adults benefit from interventions, or therapies, that can reduce symptoms and increase skills and abilities. Although it is best to begin intervention as soon as possible, the benefits of therapy can continue throughout life.

Social Challenges

Communication Difficulties

Repetitive Behaviors

Physical and Medical Issues that may Accompany Autism

Social Challenges

Typically developing infants are social by nature. They gaze at faces, turn toward voices, grasp a finger and even smile by 2 to 3 months of age. By contrast, most children who develop autism have difficulty engaging in the give-and-take of everyday human interactions. By 8 to 10 months of age, many infants who go on to develop autism are showing some symptoms such as failure to respond to their names, reduced interest in people and delayed babbling. By toddlerhood, many children with autism have difficulty playing social games, don't imitate the actions of others and prefer to play alone. They may fail to seek comfort or respond to parents' displays of anger or affection in typical ways.

Research suggests that children with autism *are* attached to their parents. However the way they express this attachment can be unusual. To parents, it may seem as if their child is disconnected. Both children and adults with autism also tend to have difficulty interpreting what others are thinking and feeling. Subtle social cures such as a smile, wave or grimace may convey little meaning. To a person who misses these social cues, a statement like "Come here!" may mean the same thing, regardless of whether the speaker is smiling and extending her arms for a hug or frowning and planting her fists on her hips. Without the ability to interpret gestures and facial expressions, the social world can seem bewildering.

Many persons with autism have similar difficulty seeing things from another person's perspective. Most five year olds understand that other people have different thoughts, feelings and goals than they have. A person with autism may lack such understanding. This, in turn, can interfere with the ability to predict or understand another person's actions.

It is common – but not universal – for those with autism to have difficulty regulating emotions. This can take the form of seemingly "immature" behavior such as crying or having outbursts in inappropriate situations. It can also lead to disruptive and physically aggressive behavior. The tendency to "lose control" may be particularly pronounced in unfamiliar, overwhelming or frustrating situations. Frustration can also result in self-injurious behaviors such as head banging, hair pulling or self-biting.

back to top

Communication Difficulties

By age three, most children have passed predictable milestones on the path to learning language. One of the earliest is babbling. By the first birthday, most typically developing toddlers say a word or two, turn and look when they hear their names, point to objects they want or want to show to someone (not all cultures use pointing in this way). When offered something distasteful, they can make clear – by sound or expression – that the answer is "no."

By contrast, young children with autism tend to be delayed in babbling and speaking and learning to use gestures. Some infants who later develop autism coo and babble during the first few months of life before losing these communicative behaviors. Others experience significant language delays and don't begin to speak until much later. With therapy, however, most people with autism do learn to use spoken language and all can learn to communicate.

Many nonverbal or nearly nonverbal children and adults learn to use communication systems such as pictures (image at left), sign language, electronic word processors or even speech-generating devices.

Visual Supports and Autism Spectrum Disorders

When language begins to develop, the person with autism may use speech in unusual ways. Some have difficulty combining words into meaningful sentences. They may speak only single words or repeat the same phrase over and over. Some go through a stage where they repeat what they hear verbatim (echolalia).

Some mildly affected children exhibit only slight delays in language or even develop precocious language and unusually large vocabularies – yet have difficulty sustaining a conversation. Some children and adults with autism tend to carry on monologues on a favorite subject, giving others little chance to comment. In other words, the ordinary "give and take" of conversation proves difficult. Some children with ASD with superior language skills tend to speak like little professors, failing to pick up on the "kid-speak" that's common among their peers.

Another common difficulty is the inability to understand body language, tone of voice and expressions that aren't meant to be taken literally. For example, even an adult with autism might interpret a sarcastic "Oh, that's just great!" as meaning it really is great.

Conversely, someone affected by autism may not exhibit typical body language. Facial expressions, movements and gestures may not match what they are saying. Their tone of voice may fail to reflect their feelings. Some use a high-pitched sing-song or a flat, robot-like voice. This can make it difficult for others know what they want and need. This failed communication, in turn, can lead to frustration and inappropriate behavior (such as screaming or grabbing) on the part of the person with autism. Fortunately, there are proven methods for helping children and adults with autism learn better ways to express their needs. As the person with autism learns to communicate what he or she wants, challenging behaviors often subside. (See section on Treatments.)

Repetitive Behaviors

Unusual repetitive behaviors and/or a tendency to engage in a restricted range of activities are another core symptom of autism. Common repetitive behaviors include hand-flapping, rocking, jumping and twirling, arranging and rearranging objects, and repeating sounds, words, or phrases. Sometimes the repetitive behavior is self-stimulating, such as wiggling fingers in front of the eyes.

The tendency to engage in a restricted range of activities can be seen in the way that many children with autism play with toys. Some spend hours lining up toys in a specific way instead of using them for pretend play. Similarly, some adults are preoccupied with having household or other objects in a fixed order or place. It can prove extremely upsetting if someone or something disrupts the order. Along these lines many children and adults with autism need and demand extreme consistency in their environment and daily routine. Slight changes can be extremely stressful and lead to outbursts

Repetitive behaviors can take the form of intense preoccupations, or obsessions. These extreme interests can prove all the more unusual for their content (e.g. fans, vacuum cleaners or toilets) or depth of knowledge (e.g. knowing and repeating astonishingly detailed information about Thomas the Tank Engine or astronomy). Older children and adults with autism may develop tremendous interest in numbers, symbols, dates or science topics.

back to top

Associated Medical Conditions

Thanks to donor support, Autism Speaks continues to fund research into the causes and treatment of the medical conditions associated with ASD. You can explore these studies here. This research is reflected in the comprehensive care model at the heart of our Autism Treatment Network(ATN) clinics. To find out if there is an ATN clinic close to you, click here. For in depth information on medical conditions, please see our website's related pages: "Treatments for Associated Medical Conditions" and "What Treatments are Available for Speech, Language and Motor Impairments," in addition to the information below.

Genetic Disorders

Some children with autism have an identifiable genetic condition that affects brain development. These genetic disorders include Fragile X syndrome, Angelman syndrome, tuberous sclerosis and chromosome 15 duplication syndrome and other single-gene and chromosomal disorders. While further study is needed, single gene disorders appear to affect 15 to 20 percent of those with ASD. Some of these syndromes have characteristic features or family histories, the presence of which may prompt your doctor to refer to a geneticist or neurologist for further testing. The results can help guide treatment, awareness of associated medical issues and life planning.

Gastrointestinal (GI) Disorders

GI distress is common among persons with autism, and affects up to 85 percent of children with ASD. These conditions range in severity from a tendency for chronic constipation or diarrhea to inflammatory bowel disease. Pain caused by GI issues can prompt behavioral changes such as increased self soothing (rocking, head banging, etc) or outbursts of aggression or self-injury. Conversely, appropriate treatment can improve behavior and quality of life. Please see our treatment section on "Gastrointestinal Disorders." It includes discussion of popular dietary interventions. Thanks to donor support, Autism Speaks continues to fund research into causes and treatments.

Seizure Disorders

Seizure disorders, including epilepsy, occur in as many as 39 percent of those with autism. It is more common in people with autism who also have intellectual disability than those without. Someone with autism may experience more than one type of seizure. The easiest to recognize is the grand mal, or tonic-clonic, seizure. Others include "petit mal" seizures (when a person temporarily appears "absent") and subclinical seizures, which may be apparent only with electroencephalogram (EEG) testing.

Seizures associated with autism tend to start in either early childhood or adolescence. But they may occur at any time. If you are concerned that you or your child may be having seizures, it is important to raise the issue with your doctor for possible referral to a neurologist for further evaluation.

Sleep Dysfunction

Sleep problems are common among children and adolescents with autism and may likewise affect many adults. For more information and helpful guidance, see our ATN Sleep Strategies Tool Kit (available for free download).

Sensory Processing Problems

Many persons with autism have unusual responses to sensory input. They have difficulty processing and integrating sensory information, or stimuli, such as sights, sounds smells, tastes and/or movement. They may experience seemingly ordinary stimuli as painful, unpleasant or confusing. (Explore our donor-funded research on causes and treatments here.)

Some of those with autism are hypersensitive to sounds or touch, a condition also known as sensory defensiveness. Others are under-responsive, or hyposensitive. An example of hypersensitivity would be the inability to tolerate wearing clothing, being touched or being in a room with normal lighting. Hyposensitivity can include failure to respond when one's name is called. Many sensory processing problems can be addressed with occupational therapy and/or sensory integration therapy. (More information on these therapies, here.)

Pica

Pica is a tendency to eat things that are not food. Eating non-food items is a normal part of development between the ages of 18 and 24 months. However, some children and adults with autism and other developmental disabilities continue to eat items such as dirt, clay, chalk or paint chips. For this reason, it is important to test for elevated blood levels of lead in those who persistently mouth fingers or objects that might be contaminated with this common environmental toxin.

How Is Autism Treated?

Image Courtesy UNC Medical Center

Each child or adult with autism is unique and, so, each autism intervention plan should be tailored to address specific needs.

Intervention can involve behavioral treatments, medicines or both. Many persons with autism have additional medical conditions such as sleep disturbance, seizures and gastrointestinal (GI) distress. Addressing these conditions can improve attention, learning and related behaviors. (Learn more about Treatment of Autism's Core Symptoms and Treatment of Associated Medical Conditions.)

Early intensive behavioral intervention involves a child's entire family, working closely with a team of professionals. In some early intervention programs, therapists come into the home to deliver services. This can include parent training with the parent leading therapy sessions under the supervision of the therapist. Other programs deliver therapy in a specialized center, classroom or preschool. (Learn more about Early Intervention.)

Typically, different interventions and supports become appropriate as a child develops and acquires social and learning skills. As children with autism enter school, for example, they may benefit from targeted social skills training and specialized approaches to teaching.

Adolescents with autism can benefit from transition services that promote a successful maturation into independence and employment opportunities of adulthood. (Learn more about Transition in our Transition Tool Kit.)

What Early Intervention Therapies Are Currently Available?

Objective scientific studies have confirmed the benefits of two methods of comprehensive behavioral early intervention. They are the Lovaas Model based on Applied Behavior Analysis (ABA) and the Early Start Denver Model. Parents and therapists also report success with other commonly used behavioral therapies, including Floortime, Pivotal Response Therapy and Verbal Behavior Therapy. For still more information, also see the "Treatment and Therapies" chapter of our 100 Day Kit.

Treatment Options for Toddlers and Preschool Children

Scientific studies have demonstrated that early intensive behavioral intervention improves learning, communication and social skills in young children with autism. While the outcomes of early intervention vary, all children benefit. Researchers have developed a number of effective early intervention models. They vary in details, but all good early intervention programs share certain features. They include:

√ The child receives structured, therapeutic activities for at least 25 hours per week.

√ Highly trained therapists and/or teachers deliver the intervention. Well-trained paraprofessionals may assist with the intervention under the supervision of an experienced professional with expertise in autism therapy.

√ The therapy is guided by specific and well-defined learning objectives, and the child's progress in meeting these objectives is regularly evaluated and recorded.

√ The intervention focuses on the core areas affected by autism. These include social skills, language and communication, imitation, play skills, daily living and motor skills.

√ The program provides the child with opportunities to interact with typically developing peers.

√ The program actively engages parents in the intervention, both in decision making and the delivery of treatment.

√ The therapists make clear their respect for the unique needs, values and perspectives of the child and his or her family.

√ The program involves a multidisciplinary team that includes, as needed, a physician, speech-language pathologist and occupational therapist.

Do Children or Adults Diagnosed with Autism Ever Move Off "the Spectrum"?

Growing evidence suggests that a small minority of persons with autism progress to the point where they no longer meet the criteria for a diagnosis of autism spectrum disorder (ASD). Various theories exist as to why this happens. They include the possibility of an initial misdiagnosis, the possibility that some children mature out of certain forms of autism and the possibility that successful treatment can, in some instances, produce outcomes that no longer meet the criteria for an autism diagnosis.

You may also hear about children diagnosed with autism who reach "best outcome" status. This means they have scored within normal ranges on tests for IQ, language, adaptive functioning, school placement and personality, but still have mild symptoms on some personality and diagnostic tests.

Some children who no longer meet the criteria for a diagnosis of autism spectrum disorder are later diagnosed with attention deficit and hyperactivity disorder (ADHD), anxiety disorder or a relatively high-functioning form of autism such as Asperger Syndrome.

Currently, we don't know what percentage of persons with autism will progress to the point where they "lose their diagnosis." We likewise need further research to determine what genetic, physiological or developmental factors might predict who will achieve such outcomes.

We do know that significant improvement in autism symptoms is most often reported in connection with intensive early intervention—though at present, we cannot predict which children will have such responses to therapy.

We also know that many people with autism go on to live independent and fulfilling lives, and that *all* deserve the opportunity to work productively, develop meaningful and fulfilling relationships and enjoy life. With better interventions and supports available, those affected by autism are having better outcomes in all spheres of life.

For more information and resources, please see our Video Glossary and FAQs and special sections on Symptoms, Diagnosis, Learn the Signs, Your Child's Rights, Asperger Syndrome and PDD-NOS. We also offer a number of resource-packed tool kits for free download from our Family Services Tool Kits page and our Autism Treatment Network Tools You Can Use page). Our 100 Day Kit is for families who have a child recently diagnosed with autism. *These resources are made possible through the generous support of our families, volunteers and other donors, as well as through grants administered by the National Institutes of Health.*

Autism & Your Family

How will I deal with this diagnosis?

Stages Associated with Grieving

Caring for the Caregiver

Fifteen Tips for Your Family

How will I deal with this diagnosis?

It's not easy to hear the news that your child has autism, and realize that your life will be utterly different than you had expected it to be. Daily life with a special-needs child presents many unique challenges. How do you come to terms with the fact that your child has autism? How do you cope once you get over the initial shock? We aim to help you by providing regular features on topics ranging from how autism affects your family to day-to-day survival strategies.

You are never prepared for a diagnosis of autism. It is likely that you will experience a range of emotions. It is painful to love so much, to want something so much, and not quite get it. You want your child to get better so much you may feel some of the stages commonly associated with grieving. You may "revisit" these feelings from time to time in the future. Part of moving forward, is dealing with your own needs and emotions along the way.

Stages Associated with Grieving

Shock

Immediately after the diagnosis you may feel stunned or confused. The reality of the diagnosis may be so overwhelming that you're not ready to accept it or you initially ignore it. You may also question the diagnosis or search for another doctor who will tell you something different.

Sadness or Grief

Many parents must mourn some of the hopes and dreams they held for their child before they can move on. There will probably be many times when you feel extremely sad. Friends may refer to this as being "depressed," which can sound frightening.

There is, however, a difference between sadness and depression. Depression often stands in the way of moving forward. Allowing yourself to feel sadness can help you grow. You have every right to feel sad and to express it in ways that are comfortable. Crying can help release some of the tension that builds up when you try to hold in sadness. A good cry can get you over one hurdle and help you face the next.

Anger

With time, your sadness may give way to anger. Although anger is a natural part of the process, you may find that it's directed at those closest to you – your child, your spouse, your friend or at the world in general. You may also feel resentment toward parents of typical children. Your anger may come out in different ways – snapping at people, overreacting at small things, even screaming and yelling. Anger is normal. It is a healthy and expected reaction to feelings of loss and stress that come with this diagnosis. Expressing your anger releases tension. It's an attempt to tell the people around you that you hurt, that you are outraged that this diagnosis has happened to your child.

Denial

You may go through periods of refusing to believe what is happening to your child. You don't consciously choose this reaction; like anger, it just happens. During this time, you may not be able to hear the facts as they related to your child's diagnosis. Don't be critical of yourself for reacting this way. Denial is a way of coping. It may be what gets you through a particularly difficult period. You must, however, be aware of that you may be experiencing denial so that it doesn't cause you to lose focus on your child's treatment.

Try not to "shoot the messenger."

When someone, a professional, a therapist or a teacher, tells you something that is hard to hear about your child, consider that they are trying to help you so that you can address the problem. It is important not to alienate people who can give you helpful feedback and monitoring of your child's progress. Whether you agree or not, try to thank them for the information. If you are upset, try considering their information when you have had a chance to calm down.

Loneliness

You may feel isolated and lonely. These feelings may have many causes. Loneliness may also come from the fact that in your new situation you simply don't feel you have the time to contact friends or family for company or that, if you did reach out, they wouldn't understand or be supportive. In the pages that follow, we have some suggestions for taking care of yourself and for getting the support you need.

Acceptance

Ultimately, you may feel a sense of acceptance. It's helpful to distinguish between accepting that your child has been diagnosed with autism and accepting autism. Accepting the diagnosis simply means that you are ready to advocate for your child.
The period following an autism diagnosis can be very challenging, even for the most harmonious families. Although the child affected by autism may never experience the negative emotions associated with the diagnosis, parents, siblings and extended family members may each process the diagnosis in different ways, and at different rates.

Give yourself time to adjust

Be patient with yourself. It will take some time to understand your child's disorder and the impact it has on you and your family. Difficult emotions may resurface from time to time. There may be times when you feel helpless and angry that autism has resulted in a life that is much different than you had planned. But you will also experience feelings of hope as your child begins to make progress.

Caring for the Caregiver

Changing the course of your child's life with autism can be a very rewarding experience. You are making an enormous difference in his or her life. To make it happen, you need to take care of yourself. Take a moment to answer these questions: Where does your support and strength come from? How are you really doing? Do you need to cry? Complain? Scream? Would you like some help but don't know who to ask?

"Remember that if you want to take the best possible care of your child, you must first take the best possible care of yourself."

Parents often fail to evaluate their own sources of strength, coping skills, or emotional attitudes. You may be so busy meeting the needs of your child that you don't allow yourself time to relax, cry, or simply think. You may wait until you are so exhausted or stressed out that you can barely carry on before you consider your own needs. Reaching this point is bad for you and for your family.

You may feel that your child needs you right now, more than ever. Your "to do" list may be what is driving you forward right now. Or, you may feel completely overwhelmed and not know here to start. There is no single way to cope. Each family is unique and deals with stressful situations differently. Getting your child started in treatment will help you feel better.

Acknowledging the emotional impact of autism and taking care of yourself during this stressful period will help prepare you for the challenges ahead.

Autism is a pervasive, multi-faceted disorder. It will not only change the way that you look at your child, it will change the way you look at the world. As some parents may tell you, you may be a better person for it. The love and hope that you have for your child is probably stronger than you realize.

Here are some tips from parents who have experienced what you are going through:

Get going.

Getting your child started in treatment will help. There are many details you will be managing in an intensive treatment program, especially if it is based in your home. If you know your child is engaged in meaningful activities, you will be more able to focus on moving forward. It may also free up some of your time so you can educate yourself, advocate for your child, and take care of yourself so that you can keep going.

Ask for help.

Asking for help can be very difficult, especially at first. Don't hesitate to use whatever support is available to you. People around you may want to help, but may not know how. Is there someone who can take your other kids somewhere for an afternoon? Or cook dinner for your family one night so that you can spend the time learning: Can they pick a few things up for you at the store or do a load of laundry? Can they let other people know you are going through a difficult time and could use a hand?

Talk to someone.

Everyone needs someone to talk to. Let someone know what you are going through and how you feel. Someone who just listens can be a great source of strength. If you can't get out of the house, use the phone to call a friend. Link to Family Services

"At my support group I met a group of women who were juggling the same things I am. It felt so good not to feel like I was from another planet!"

Consider joining a support group.

It may be helpful to listen or talk to people who have been or are going through a similar experience. Support groups can be great sources for information about what services are available in your area and who provides them. You may have to try more than one to find a group that feels right to you. You may find you aren't a "support group kind of person." For many parents in your situation, support groups provide valuable hope, comfort and encouragement. Link to AS Support Network

Try to take a break.

If you can, allow yourself to take some time away, even if it is only a few minutes to take a walk. If it's possible, getting out to a movie, going shopping, or visiting a friend can make a world of difference. If you feel guilty about taking a break, try to remind yourself that it will help you to be renewed for the things you need to do when you get back.

Try to get some rest. If you are getting regular sleep, you will be better prepared to make good decisions, be more patient with your child and deal with the stress in your life.

Consider keeping a journal.

Louise DeSalvo, in *Writing as a Way of Healing*, notes that studies have shown that "writing that describes traumatic events and our deepest thoughts and feelings about them is linked with improved immune function, improved emotional and physical health," and positive behavioral changes. Some parents have found a journaling a helpful tool for keeping track of their children's progress, what's working and what isn't.

Be mindful of the time you spend on the Internet. The Internet will be one of the most important tools you have for learning what you need to know about autism and how to help your child.

Unfortunately, there is more information on the web than any of us have time to read in a lifetime. There may also be a lot of misinformation. Right now, while you are trying to make the most of every minute, keep an eye on the clock and frequently ask yourself these important questions:

• Is what I'm reading right now very likely to be relevant to my child?

• Is it new information?

• Is it helpful?

• Is it from a reliable source?

Sometimes, the time you spend on the Internet will be incredibly valuable. Other times, it may be better for you and your child if you use that time to take care of yourself.

Fifteen Tips for Your Family

As a result of her work with many families who deal so gracefully with the challenges of autism, Family Therapist, Kathryn Smerling, Ph.D., offers these five tips for parents, five for siblings and five for extended family members:

<u>5 Tips for Parents</u>

Learn to be the best advocate you can be for your child.

Be informed. Take advantage of all the services that are available to you in your community. You will meet practitioners and providers who can educate you and help you. You will gather great strength from the people you meet.

Don't push your feelings away.

Talk about them. You may feel both ambivalent and angry. Those are emotions to be expected. It's OK to feel conflicting emotions. Try to direct your anger towards the disorder and not towards your loved ones. When you find yourself arguing with your spouse over an autism related issue, try to remember that this topic is painful for both of you; and be careful not to get mad at each other when it really is the autism that has you so upset and angry.

an Autism Awareness Anthology

Try to have some semblance of an adult life.

Be careful to not let autism consume every waking hour of your life. Spend quality time with your typically developing children and your spouse, and refrain from constantly talking about autism. Everyone in your family needs support, and to be happy despite the circumstances.

Appreciate the small victories your child may achieve.

Love your child and take great pride in each small accomplishment. Focus on what they can do instead of making comparisons with a typically developing child. Love them for who they are rather than what they should be.

Get involved with the Autism community.

Don't underestimate the power of "community". You may be the captain of your team, but you can't do everything yourself. Make friends with other parents who have children with autism. By meeting other parents you will have the support of families who understand your day to day challenges. Getting involved with autism advocacy is empowering and productive. You will be doing something for yourself as well as your child by being proactive.

5 Tips for Brothers & Sisters

Remember that you are not alone!

Every family is confronted with life's challenges... and yes, autism is challenging... but, if you look closely, nearly everyone has something difficult to face in their families.

Be proud of your brother or sister.

Learn to talk about autism and be open and comfortable describing the disorder to others. If you are comfortable with the topic…they will be comfortable too. If you are embarrassed by your brother or sister, your friends will sense this and it will make it awkward for them. If you talk openly to your friends about autism, they will become comfortable. But, like everyone else, sometimes you will love your brother or sister, and sometimes you will hate them. It's okay to feel your feelings. And, often it's easier when you have a professional counselor to help you understand them – someone special who is here just for you!

Love your brother or sister the way they are.

While it is OK to be sad that you have a brother or sister affected by autism it doesn't help to be upset and angry for extended periods of time. Your anger doesn't change the situation; it only makes you unhappier. Remember your Mom and Dad may have those feelings too.

Spend time with your Mom and Dad alone.

Doing things together as a family with and without your brother or sister strengthens your family bond. It's OK for you to want alone time. Having a family member with autism can often be very time consuming, and attention grabbing. You need to feel important too. Remember, even if your brother or sister didn't have autism, you would still need alone time with Mom and Dad.

Find an activity you can do with your brother or sister.

You will find it rewarding to connect with your brother or sister, even if it is just putting a simple puzzle together. No matter how impaired they may be, doing something together creates a closeness. They will look forward to these shared activities and greet you with a special smile.

5 Tips for Grandparents and Extended Family

Family members have a lot to offer.

Each family member is able to offer the things they have learned to do best over time. Ask how you can be helpful to your family.

Your efforts will be appreciated whether it means taking care of the child so that the parents can go out to dinner, or raising money for the special school that helps your family's child. Organize a lunch, a theatre benefit, a carnival, or a card game. It will warm your family's hearts to know that you are pitching in to create support and closeness.

Seek out your own support.

If you find yourself having a difficult time accepting and dealing with the fact that your loved one has autism, seek out your own support. Your family may not be able to provide you with that kind of support so you must be considerate and look elsewhere. In this way you can be stronger for them, helping with the many challenges they face.

Be open and honest about the disorder.

The more you talk about the matter, the better you will feel. Your friends and family can become your support system...but only if you share your thoughts with them. It may be hard to talk about it at first, but as time goes on it will be easier. In the end your experience with autism will end up teaching you and your family profound life lessons.

Put judgment aside.

Consider your family's feelings and be supportive. Respect the decisions they make for their child with autism. They are working very hard to explore and research all options, and are typically coming to well thought out conclusions. Try not to compare children (this goes for typically developing kids as well). Children with autism can be brought up to achieve their personal best.

Learn more about Autism.

It affects people of all social and economic standing. There is promising research, with many possibilities for the future. Share that sense of hope with your family while educating yourself about the best ways to help manage this disorder.

Carve out special time for each child.

You can enjoy special moments with both typically developing family members and the family member with autism. Yes, they may be different but both children look forward to spending time with you. Children with autism thrive on routines, so find one thing that you can do together that is structured, even if it is simply going to a park for fifteen minutes.

an Autism Awareness Anthology

If you go to the same park every week, chances are over time that activity will become easier and easier…it just takes time and patience. If you are having a difficult time trying to determine what you can do, ask your family. They will sincerely appreciate that you are making.

Facts about Autism

Did you know ...

- Autism now affects 1 in 88 children and 1 in 54 boys
- Autism prevalence figures are growing
- Autism is the fastest-growing serious developmental disability in the U.S.
- Autism costs a family $60,000 a year on average
- Autism receives less than 5% of the research funding of many less prevalent childhood diseases
- Boys are nearly five times more likely than girls to have autism
- There is no medical detection or cure for autism

National Institutes of Health Funds Allocation

- Total 2012 NIH budget: $30.86 billion
- Of this, only $169 million goes directly to autism research. This represents 0.55% of total NIH funding.

an Autism Awareness Anthology

Asperger's Syndrome

John Elder Robison, a member of Autism Speaks Scientific Advisory Board, describes his experience learning about and living with Asperger's Syndrome, which he also details evocatively in his books Look Me in the Eye: My Life with Asperger's *and* Be Different: Adventures of a Free-Range Aspergian.

What Is Asperger's Syndrome?

Asperger Syndrome is an autism spectrum disorder (ASD) considered to be on the "high functioning" end of the spectrum. Affected children and adults have difficulty with social interactions and exhibit a restricted range of interests and/or repetitive behaviors. Motor development may be delayed, leading to clumsiness or uncoordinated motor movements. Compared with those affected by other forms of ASD, however, those with Asperger syndrome do not have significant delays or difficulties in language or cognitive development. Some even demonstrate precocious vocabulary – often in a highly specialized field of interest.

The following behaviors are often associated with Asperger syndrome. However, they are seldom all present in any one individual and vary widely in degree:

- limited or inappropriate social interactions

- "robotic" or repetitive speech

- challenges with nonverbal communication (gestures, facial expression, etc.) coupled with average to above average verbal skills

- tendency to discuss self rather than others

- inability to understand social/emotional issues or nonliteral phrases

- lack of eye contact or reciprocal conversation

- obsession with specific, often unusual, topics

- one-sided conversations

- awkward movements and/or mannerisms

How is Asperger Syndrome diagnosed?

Asperger syndrome often remains undiagnosed until a child or adult begins to have serious difficulties in school, the workplace or their personal lives. Indeed, many adults with Asperger syndrome receive their diagnosis when seeking help for related issues such as anxiety or depression. Diagnosis tends to center primarily on difficulties with social interactions.

Children with Asperger syndrome tend to show typical or even exceptional language development. However, many tend to use their language skills inappropriately or awkwardly in conversations or social situations such as interacting with their peers. Often, the symptoms of Asperger syndrome are confused with those of other behavioral issues such as attention deficit and hyperactivity disorder (ADHD). Indeed, many persons affected by Asperger syndrome are initially diagnosed with ADHD until it becomes clear that their difficulties stem more from an inability to socialize than an inability to focus their attention.

For instance, someone with Asperger syndrome might initiate conversations with others by extensively relating facts related to a particular topic of interest. He or she may resist discussing anything else and have difficulty allowing others to speak. Often, they don't notice that others are no longer listening or are uncomfortable with the topic. They may lack the ability to "see things" from the other person's perspective.

Another common symptom is an inability to understand the intent behind another person's actions, words and behaviors. So children and adults affected by Asperger syndrome may miss humor and other implications. Similarly, they may not instinctually respond to such "universal" nonverbal cues such as a smile, frown or "come here" motion.

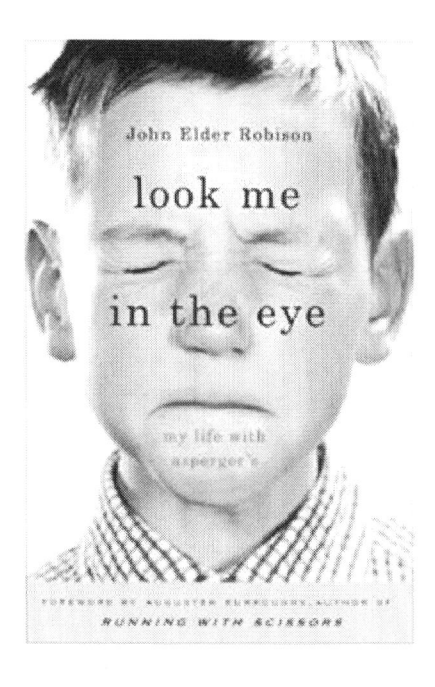

John Elder Robison — look me in the eye: my life with asperger's

For these reasons, social interactions can seem confusing and overwhelming to individuals with Asperger syndrome. Difficulties in seeing things from another person's perspective can make it extremely difficult to predict or understand the actions of others. They may not pick up on what is or isn't appropriate in a particular situation. For instance, someone with Asperger syndrome might speak too loudly when entering a church service or a room with a sleeping baby – and not understand when "shushed."

Some individuals with Asperger syndrome have a peculiar manner of speaking. This can involve speaking overly loud, in a monotone or with an unusual intonation. It is also common, but not universal, for people with Asperger syndrome to have difficulty controlling their emotions. They may cry or laugh easily or at inappropriate times.

Another common, but not universal, sign is an awkwardness or delay in motor skills. As children, in particular, they may have difficulties on the playground because they can't catch a ball or understand how to swing on the monkey bars despite their peers' repeated attempts to teach them.

Not all individuals with Asperger syndrome display all of these behaviors. In addition, each of these symptoms tends to vary widely among affected individuals.

It is very important to note that the challenges presented by Asperger Syndrome are very often accompanied by unique gifts. Indeed, a remarkable ability for intense focus is a common trait.

What kinds of services and supports are there for individuals affected by Asperger Syndrome?

There is no single or best treatment for Asperger syndrome. Many adults diagnosed with Asperger syndrome find cognitive behavioral therapy particularly helpful in learning social skills and self-control of emotions, obsessions and repetitive behaviors.

A social skills training class for teens at the Carolina Institute for Developmental Disabilities.

Educational and social support programs for children with Asperger syndrome generally teach social and adaptive skills step by step using highly structured activities. The instructor may repeat important ideas or instructions to help reinforce more adaptive behaviors. Many of these programs also involve parent training so that lessons can be continued in the home. Like adults, many children find cognitive behavioral therapy helpful.

Group programs can be particularly helpful for social skills training. Speech and language therapy – either in a group or one on one with a therapist can likewise help with conversation skills. Many children with Asperger syndrome also benefit from occupational and physical therapy.

Most experts feel that the earlier interventions are started, the better the outcome. However, many persons who receive their diagnosis as adults make great strides by coupling their new awareness with counseling.

In addition to behavioral interventions, some persons affected by Asperger syndrome are helped by medications such as selective serotonin reuptake inhibitors (SSRIs), antipsychotics and stimulants to treat associated problems such as anxiety, depression and hyperactivity and ADHD.

With increased self-awareness and therapy, many children and adults learn to cope with the challenges of Asperger syndrome. Social interaction and personal relationships may remain difficult. However, many affected adults work successfully in mainstream jobs, and some make great contributions to society.

an Autism Awareness Anthology

How has our understanding of Asperger Syndrome evolved?

In 1944, an Austrian pediatrician named Hans Asperger described four young patients with similar social difficulties. Although their intelligence appeared normal, the children lacked nonverbal communication skills and failed to demonstrate empathy with their peers. Their manner of speech was either disjointed or overly formal, and their all-absorbing interests in narrow topics dominated their conversations. The children also shared a tendency to be clumsy.

Photo of Temple Grandin, courtesy Christopher Gauthiér

Dr. Asperger's observations, published in German, remained little known until 1981. In that year, the English physician Lorna Wing published a series of case studies of children with similar symptoms. Wing's writings on "Asperger syndrome" were widely published and popularized. In 1994, Asperger syndrome was added to the fourth edition of the Diagnostic and Statistical Manual of Mental Disorders (DSM-4), the American Psychiatric Association's diagnostic reference book.

There can be considerable overlap in the diagnostic symptoms of Asperger and that of other forms of ASD among children and adults who have normal intelligence and no significant language delay. So-called "high functioning autism" and Asperger syndrome share similar challenges and benefit from similar treatment approaches.

In recent years, such high profile authors and speakers as John Elder Robison and animal scientist Temple Grandin have shared their stories of life with Asperger syndrome. In doing so, they have helped raise awareness of its associated challenges and special abilities.

Asperger Syndrome and Self-Advocacy

Michael John Carley, executive director of GRASP and ASTEP

Many persons affected with Asperger syndrome take pride in their special abilities. Some take offense at the suggestion that their autism needs to be "cured."

Prominent self-advocates include Michael John Carley, executive director of the Global and Regional Asperger Syndrome Partnership (GRASP) and the Asperger Syndrome Training and Employment Program (ASTEP), and self-described "Aspergian" John Elder Robison.

Mr. Robison eloquently describes his take on the wider autism self-advocacy movement in the following excerpt from an article he wrote in Psychology Today.

"Autism is a communication disorder, with a broad range of affect. Some people's autism makes them eccentric and geeky. Other people can't speak at all, as a result of more severe autistic disability.

Therefore, in the world of autism, some of the population is capable of what some call self-advocacy while another part is not. It should come as no surprise that those groups would have very different wants and needs. That disunity of need and purpose is a fundamental issue we must address.

At its heart, self-advocacy is nothing more than speaking up to get what you want. Everyone who communicates does this, all the time. We self-advocate when we ask for different courses in college. We self-advocate when we ask for a chair with a lumbar support at work. ...

You may believe your own communication problems will be reduced if the people around you are willing to change their style of engagement to accommodate you, or you may ask that they excuse some of your expressions, which might otherwise be offensive or unacceptable.

Those are all examples of what we call self-advocacy, because the speaker is asking for what he thinks he needs to be successful."

For more information and resources, please see our Asperger Syndrome Tool Kit for families and this website's special sections on Diagnosis, Symptoms, Learn the Signs, Treatment, Your Child's Rights and PDD-NOS. These resources are made possible through the generous support of our families, volunteers and other donors.

an Autism Awareness Anthology

World Autism Awareness Day

World Autism Awareness Day

The sixth annual World Autism Awareness Day is April 2, 2013. Every year, autism organizations around the world celebrate the day with unique fundraising and awareness-raising events. How will you celebrate? To share your events, please "Like" the World Autism Awareness Day page on Facebook and submit your events by posting the information on the wall.

Autism Speaks would like to thank the Empire State Building for the special lighting last year on the evening of April 2 in celebration of the fifth annual United Nations World Autism Awareness Day on April 2nd. Learn more about the Empire State Building at www.esbnyc.com. The Empire State Building design is a trademark of ESBC and is used with permission.

Resources

For more information on Autism Spectrum Disorder please visit the following websites.

Please get informed, different doesn't mean less.

WIKIPEDIA
The Free Encyclopedia

http://en.wikipedia.org/wiki/Autism

http://www.coloredmymind.com

an Autism Awareness Anthology

HOLLYROD FOUNDATION

http://www.hollyrod.org/

AUTISM SPEAKS
It's time to listen.

http://www.autismspeaks.org

PUZZLED ~ When the Pieces don't see to Fit

https://www.facebook.com/heyjude06?ref=hl

https://www.facebook.com/AutismAwarenessPage?fref=ts

http://specialneedslove.net/

http://learningneverstops.wordpress.com/2012/10/14/autism_personal_definition/

http://forfacesofautism.org

an Autism Awareness Anthology

Literature on . . .
Autism Spectrum Disorder

Thinking in Pictures
Dr. Temple Grandin PH.D

Autism and the God Connection
William Stillman

Teaching Children with High Functioning Autism: Strategies for the Inclusive Classroom
Claire Hughes-Lynch

Love, Tears and Autism
Cecily Patterson

The Out of Sync Child: Recognizing and Coping with Sensory Processing Disorder
Carol Kranowitz and Lucy Jane Miller

Books for Children

I am Utterly Unique: Celebrating the Strengths of Children with Asperger Syndrome and High Functioning Autism

Elaine Marie Larson

Point to Happy

Miriam Smith and Afton Fraser

Troy's Amazing Universe Series

S. Kennedy Tosten

My Brother Charlie

Holly Robinson-Peete and Ryan Elizabeth Peete

an Autism Awareness Anthology

Acknowledgements

Book Cover Art

Anna Surface
Surface and Surface Photography

Anna Surface is a Kansas based photographer with an adult child living with Autism. Her photography captures a variety of themes synonymous with the Kansas Prairies and Flint Hills.

Anna's art work is featured on her company website: www.surfaceandsurfacephotography.com

Cover Design Front

Jodi Lynch aka Raayn
Poet/Writer and Graphic Artist.

Graphics & Quotes

Jodi Lynch aka Raayn
Poet/Writer and Graphic Artist

Yvette Burks

Inner Child Press

Inner Child Press is a Publishing Company Founded and Operated by Writers. Our personal publishing experiences provides us an intimate understanding of the sometimes daunting challenges Writers, New and Seasoned may face in the Business of Publishing and Marketing their Creative "Written Work".

For more Information

Inner Child Press

www.innerchildpress.com

intouch@innerchildpress.com

Made in the USA
Lexington, KY
23 February 2019